Junior Worldmark Encyclopedia of World Holidays

Junior Worldmark Encyclopedia of World Holidays

VOLUME **2**

Easter,
Halloween and
Festivals of the Dead

U·X·L

AN IMPRINT OF THE GALE GROUP

DETROIT · NEW YORK · SAN FRANCISCO
LONDON · BOSTON · WOODBRIDGE, CT

Junior Worldmark Encyclopedia of World Holidays

Robert H. Griffin and Ann H. Shurgin

Staff

Kelle Sisung, *Contributing Editor*
Carol DeKane Nagel, *U·X·L Managing Editor*
Thomas L. Romig, *U·X·L Publisher*
Meggin Condino, *Senior Analyst, New Product Development*

Dean Dauphinais, *Senior Editor, Imaging and Multimedia Content*
Shalice Shah-Caldwell, *Permissions Associate, Text and Pictures*

Robert Duncan, *Senior Imaging Specialist*
Randy A. Bassett, *Image Database Supervisor*
Barbara J. Yarrow, *Graphic Services Manager*

Pamela A. E. Galbreath, *Senior Art Director*
Graphix Group, *Typesetting*

Rita Wimberley, *Senior Buyer*
Evi Seoud, *Assistant Manager, Composition Purchasing and Electronic Prepress*
Dorothy Maki, *Manufacturing Manager*

Printed in the United States of America
10 9 8 7 6 5 4 3 2 1

Library of Congress Cataloging-in-Publication Data

Junior worldmark encyclopedia of world holidays/ edited by Robert Griffin.
    p.   cm.
Includes bibliographical references and index.
Summary: Alphabetically arranged entries provide descriptions of celebrations around the world of some thirty holidays and festivals, including national and cultural holidays, such as Independence Day and New Year's Day, which are commemorated on different days for different reasons in a number of countries.
ISBN 0-7876-3927-3 (set). — ISBN 0-7876-3928-1 (vol. 1). — ISBN 0-7876-3929-X (vol. 2). — ISBN 0-7876-3930-3 (vol. 3). — ISBN 0-7876-3931-1 (vol. 4).
1. Holidays—Encyclopedias, Juvenile. 2. Festivals—Encyclopedias, Juvenile. [1. Holidays—Encyclopedias. 2. Festivals—Encyclopedias. 3. Encyclopedias and dictionaries.] I. Griffin, Robert H., 1951–

GT3933 .J86 2000
394.26'03—dc21
                                    00-023425

Front cover photographs (top to bottom): Krewe of Rex float reproduced by permission of Archive Photos, Inc; jack-o-lanterns, monk beating drum, and Fastnacht witches reproduced by permission of AP/Wide World Photos, Inc. Back cover photograph: Chicago Children's Choir reproduced by permission of AP/Wide World Photos, Inc.

Contents

Contents

Volume 3:

Volume 4:

Contents
by Country

Contents by Country

Reader's Guide

Ever wonder why children trick-or-treat on Halloween? How Christmas festivities in Italy differ from those in the United States? What the colors of Kwanzaa represent? When will Ramadan come this year? Who creates all those floats in the parades? The answers to these and other questions about holiday traditions and lore can be found in *Junior Worldmark Encyclopedia of World Holidays*. This four-volume set explores when, where, why, and how people from thirty countries around the world celebrate eleven different holidays.

Each chapter in *Junior Worldmark Encyclopedia of World Holidays* opens with a general overview of the featured holiday. The chapter then provides details on one to six countries that observe that holiday. Each overview and country profile is arranged into the following rubrics, allowing for quick scanning or comparisons among the countries and holidays:

- **Introduction:** Offers a brief description and useful background information on the holiday. The introduction in the overview discusses the holiday in general; the country introductions focus on how the holiday is observed in that featured country.

- **History:** Discusses the holiday's development, often from ancient origins through modern times. When a holiday was established to commemorate a historical event, such as a revolution or a nation's declaration of independence, a historical account of the event is given. When a holiday began with the rise of a religion, a discussion of the growth of the religion follows. Each holiday's general history is presented in the overview, while its development in a particular country is the focus of the country history.

- **Folklore, Legends, Stories:** Each holiday has at least a few legends and stories, folklore and superstitions associated with it. These are discussed here, along with literature commonly associated with the holiday. Traditional characters or historical tales can be found, as well as a brief synopsis of a well-known story or an excerpt from a poem. Religious holidays include excerpts or synopses of the scriptural account on which they are based. For some holidays, sidebars listing popular stories and poems are included.

- **Customs, Traditions, Ceremonies:** This section delves into the actual celebration of the holiday, from preparation for its arrival through ceremonies to bid it farewell for another year. Some of the ceremonies and traditions are religious, others are secular. Some are based on beliefs and superstitions so old that no one knows their origin, while others center around the reenactment of historical or religious events. Some are carried out on a grand scale, while others involve a quiet family ceremony. Learn how a European family celebrates a particular holiday while someone in Africa or Asia celebrates it in a very different—or sometimes very similar—way.

- **Clothing, Costumes:** Some holidays, such as Halloween and Carnival, have costumes at the heart of the celebration. For others, such as Independence Days, simply wearing the national colors is enough. In many cultures, people don traditional folk costumes for particular holidays, while others just dress in their "Sunday best." Whether it is a pair of sneakers or a six-foot feather plume, clothing and costumes play an important role in the traditions. This section will explain how people dress for the holiday and why.

- **Foods, Recipes:** What does Christmas dinner mean to an Italian family? What do Chinese youngsters snack on at New Year festivals? What is the main "Thanksgiving dinner" dish in Swaziland? This rubric details the special holiday meals shared by people within a culture. It covers the foods themselves as well as table settings, mealtime ceremonies, and the significance of eating certain foods on special days. For some holidays, picnic or festival foods are also mentioned. For most countries, a favorite holiday recipe is featured.

- **Arts, Crafts, Games:** Described here are famous works of art associated with specific holidays, as well as crafts created by different peoples in connection with the holiday, such as intricate Nativity scenes made by Italian woodcarvers and special pictures created by Chinese artists to bring good luck in the New Year. Holiday decorations and traditional games are also discussed here. Included for some holidays are crafts projects that, in addition to bringing added enjoyment by making one's own decorations, will help foster an appreciation of the art of other cultures.

- **Symbols:** Included in the holiday overviews are discussions of the symbols associated with the holiday and its celebration. A description of each symbol is given, along with its origin, meaning, and significance to the holiday.

- **Music, Dance:** Whether performing classical compositions or folk dancing in a courtyard, people all over the world love to make music and dance during their holidays. This rubric focuses on the music and dance that helps make up holiday celebrations. Some musical performances can be fiercely competitive, like the steel band contests held during Carnival in Trinidad. Others are solemn and deeply moving, like a performance of Handel's *Messiah* in a cathedral at Easter. Here learn about folk instruments, the origins of songs and dances, and famous composers or musicians from many cultures. Excerpts from songs associated with the holiday are also given.

- **Special Role of Children, Young Adults:** Children and young adults often have a special role to play in holiday celebrations. While children may simply participate in family activities during a holiday in some countries, in others children have distinct roles in parades, plays and performances, or customs. Here students can learn how children their own age celebrate holidays in nations thousands of miles away.

- **For More Information and Sources:** Print and electronic sources for further study are found at the end of each holiday overview and again at the end of each country essay. Those following the overview are general sources for the holiday, whereas the others pertain to a particular nation. Books listed should be able to be found in a library, and electronic sources are accessible on the World Wide Web.

Additionally, each chapter contains a Holiday Fact Box highlighting the themes of the specific holiday, while sprinkled throughout the set are boxes featuring recipes, activities, and more fascinating facts. One hundred twenty-five photos help bring the festivities to life. Beginning each volume is a table of contents for the entire set listing the holidays and countries featured, a table of contents by country, an explanation of how the modern calendar

developed, a calendar list of world holidays, and a words to know section. Concluding each volume is a cumulative subject index providing easy access to the holidays, countries, traditions, and topics discussed throughout *Junior Worldmark Encyclopedia of World Holidays*.

Advisory Board

Special thanks to the *Junior Worldmark Encyclopedia of World Holidays* advisors for their invaluable comments and suggestions:

- Mary Alice Anderson, Media Specialist, Winona Middle School, Winona, Minnesota.

- Ginny Ayers, Department Chair, Media Technology Services, Evanston Township High School, Evanston, Illinois.

- Jonathan Betz-Zall, Children's Librarian, Sno-Isle Regional Library System, Edmonds, Washington.

- Peter Butts, Media Specialist, East Middle School, Holland, Michigan.

Comments and Suggestions

We welcome your comments on this work as well as your suggestions for holidays to be featured in future editions of *Junior Worldmark Encyclopedia of World Holidays*. Please write: Editors, *Junior Worldmark Encyclopedia of World Holidays*, U•X•L, 27500 Drake Rd., Farmington Hills, MI 48331–3535; call toll-free: 1–800–877–4253; fax: 248–414–5043; or send e-mail via www.galegroup.com.

How the Modern Calendar Developed

The Egyptian Calendar

The earliest known calendar, that of the Egyptians, was lunar based, or calculated by the cycles of the Moon. One cycle is a lunar month, about 29.5 days in length, the time it takes the Moon to revolve once around the Earth. Although the calculations are fairly simple, reliance upon lunar months eventually leads to a problem: a lunar year, based upon 12 lunar cycles, is only 354 days. This is 11 days shorter than the solar year, the time it takes Earth to revolve once around the Sun. In any agricultural society, such as that of ancient Egypt, the solar-based seasons of the year are vitally important: they are the most reliable guide for knowing when to plow, plant, harvest, or store agricultural produce. Obviously, the discrepancy between the lunar and solar year had to be addressed.

The Egyptian solution was to rely on a solar calendar to govern civil affairs and agriculture; this was put in place around the third millennium B.C. This calendar observed the same new year's day as the older lunar one, which for the Egyptians was the day, about July 3, of the appearance on the horizon just before sunrise of the star Sirius, the "Dog Star." This event was significant for the Egyptians, for it occurred at nearly the same time the Nile River flooded each year, the key to their agricultural prosperity. The new Egyptian solar calendar also retained the division of days into months, although they were no longer based on lunar cycles. The Egyptian year in the reformed calendar contained 12 months of 30 days, with 5 days added throughout the year, bringing the total number of days to 365. It was only a fraction of a day different from the length of the solar year as determined by modern scientific means.

The Sumerian Calendar

Like the early Egyptian calendar, the ancient Sumerian calendar, developed around the twenty–seventh century B.C., was lunar. To the Sumerians, however, the Moon's cycles were apparently more significant, for they retained lunar months and a 354–day year. They made alignments with the seasons by adding extra days outside the regular calendar. (This process of adding extra days as necessary to reconcile the lunar with the solar year is called intercalation.) The calendar of the sacred city of Nippur, which became the Sumerian standard in the eighteenth century B.C., assigned names to the months, with the intercalary month designated by royal decree.

The Seven–day Week

The ancient Babylonians, a Sumerian people with a highly developed astronomy, are thought to be the first people to observe a seven-day week. The concept was probably based upon the periods between the distinct phases of the moon, which roughly correspond to seven days. The Babylonians also regarded the number seven as sacred, probably because they knew of seven principal heavenly bodies—Sun, Moon, Mars, Mercury, Jupiter, Venus, and Saturn—and saw supernatural significance in their seemingly wild movements against a backdrop of fixed stars. The days of the week were named for these principal heavenly bodies, one assigned to each day according to which governed the first hour of that day.

In addition to their lunar calendar, the Babylonians also devised a solar calendar based upon the points at which the Sun rises in relation to the constellations. This calendar is the basis for the zodiac system, the key to astrology.

From the Babylonians, the ancient Hebrews are believed to have adopted the practices of intercalation and observance of a seven-day week, probably during the time of Jewish captivity in Babylon beginning in 586 B.C. Babylonian influence may also have played a role in their observing every seventh day as special—the Jewish concept of Sabbath. Evidence for an earlier Jewish calendar (from at least the twelfth century B.C.)

does exist, however; thus, the observance of a Sabbath may well have existed before the Babylonian captivity. In any event, it is clear that the tradition of the seven-day week, as well as the retention of the concept of months, has much to do with the Western inheritance of Jewish calendar practices. (See also **The Hebrew Calendar,** below.)

The seven-day week as we know it today was carried into Christian use in the first century A.D. and was officially adopted by the Roman emperor Constantine in the fourth century. Interestingly, the English names for the days still reflect their origin in the names of the seven principal heavenly bodies of the ancient Babylonian astronomy:

- **Sunday:** Old English *Sunnan daeg,* a translation of Latin *dies solis,* "day of the sun."

- **Monday:** Old English *Monan daeg,* a translation of Latin *lunae dies,* "day of the moon"; compare with the French *lundi.*

- **Tuesday:** Old English *Tiwes daeg,* "day of Tiw," an adaptation of Latin *dies Martis,* "day of Mars" (the god Tiw being identified with the Roman Mars); compare with the French *Mardi.*

- **Wednesday:** Old English *Wodnes daeg,* "Woden's Day," an adaptation of Latin *Mercurii dies,* "day of Mercury" (the god Woden being identified with the Roman Mercury); compare with the French *mercredi.*

- **Thursday:** Old English *Thunres daeg,* "Thunor's day" or "Thor's day," an adaptation of the Latin *dies Jovis,* "day of Jove" (the god Thor being identified with the Roman Jove); compare with the French *jeudi.*

- **Friday:** Old English *Frize daeg,* "Freya's Day," an adaptation of the Latin *dies Veneris,* "day of Venus" (the goddess Freya being identified with the Roman Venus); compare with the French *vendredi.*

- **Saturday:** Old English *Saetern(es) daeg,* derived from the Latin *Saturni Dies,* "day of Saturn."

The Hebrew Calendar

Little is known of the Hebrew calendar prior to the Exodus from Egypt (c. 1250 B.C.) except that it appears to have contained four single and four double months called *yereah.* The early Hebrews apparently did not study the heavens and timekeeping as did their Sumerian and Egyptian neighbors. In fact, it was only after the period of Babylonian exile (586–516 B.C.) that a more fully developed method of timekeeping was adopted to modify the ancient practices. After their return from captivity, the Hebrews employed a calendar very similar to that of the Babylonians, intercalating (adding as necessary) months into the lunar calendar so it would correspond with the solar year. Unlike the Babylonians, who marked the beginning of the new year in the spring, the Hebrews retained the custom of recognizing the new year in the autumn, the time of their principal religious festivals of Rosh Hashanah (New Year), Yom Kippur, the Sukkoth, all falling in the month of Tishri (September/October). Still, similarities between the Jewish and Babylonian calendars are clear from a comparison of the names used in each system for the months:

Names of the Months in the Babylonian and Jewish Calendar Systems

Babylonian	Jewish	Equivalent
Nisanu	Nisan	March/April
Aiaru	Iyar	April/May
Simanu	Sivan	May/June
Du'uzu	Tammuz	June/July
Abu	Ab	July/August
Ululu	Elul	August/September
Tashritu	Tishri	September/October
Arahsamnu	Heshvan	October/November
Kislimu	Kislev	November/December
Tebetu	Tebet	December/January
Shabatu	Shebat	January/February
Adaru I	Adar	February/March
Adaru II	Veadar	(intercalary)

Thus, the year in the Jewish (and Babylonian) calendar consists of 12 lunar months, with the addition of the intercalary month as necessary to synchronize with the solar year. The months contain alternately 29 or 30 days; the beginning of each is marked by the appearance of the new moon.

The Hebrew week ends with the observation of the Sabbath, lasting from sunset Friday to sunset Saturday, a day to rest and pay homage to God. The use of weeks and observation of a day of rest are primarily contributions from Jewish tradition to our present–day calendar. (See also **The Seven–day Week**, above.)

The Jewish Era, designated *A.M.* (for Latin *anno mundi,* "year of the world"), begins with the supposed date of Creation, which tradition sets at 3761 B.C. After more than two thousand years, devout Jews still observe essentially the same calendar for religious purposes, although they follow other calendars for their business and social lives. With its roots based in scripture, the Hebrew calendar has remained a primary binding force of tradition and continuity throughout the long and varied history of the Jewish people.

The Early Roman Calendar

Ancient Rome played a significant role in the development of our modern method of reckoning time. The earliest known Roman calendar, created according to legend by the city's founder, Romulus, in the eighth century B.C., had 10 months totaling 304 days: 6 months of 30 days and 4 months of 31 days. The new year began in March, the time when agricultural activities were revived and new military campaigns were initiated, and ended with December, which was followed by a winter gap that was used for intercalation. The Etruscan king Numa Pompilius (reigned 715–673 B.C.) reformed Romulus's primitive calendar, instituting a lunar year of 12 months. The two new months, following December, were named *Januarius* and *Februarius,* and were respectively assigned 29 and 28 days.

While this reform was a clear improvement, it was set aside in Rome during a time of political unrest that began about 510 B.C. Still, its advantages were remembered, and in 153 B.C. Numa Pompilius's calendar was again adopted. At the same time the beginning of the Roman civil year was changed to January 1, which became the day that newly elected consuls assumed office.

Days of the Roman Month

The Romans did not have a method for numbering the days of their months in a series. They did, however, establish three fixed points from which other days could be reckoned. These three designations were: 1) *Kalends,* the first day of the month (ancestor of English *calendar*); 2) *Nones,* the ninth day; and 3) *Ides,* originally the day of the full moon of the lunar month. In months of 31 days (March, May, July, October) the Nones were the seventh day and the Ides the fifteenth, while in the shorter months the Nones fell on the fifth and the Ides on the thirteenth day.

The Romans also recognized a market day, called *nundinae,* which occurred every eighth day. This established a cycle for agriculture in which the farmer worked for seven days in his field and brought his produce to the city on the eighth for sale.

The Julian Calendar

It was not until the mid-first century B.C., by which time the reformed lunar calendar had shifted eight weeks out of phase with the seasons, that emperor Julius Caesar determined that a long-term and scientific reform of the calendar must take place. He enlisted the aid of the Alexandrian astronomer Sosigenes to devise the new calendar. The solar year was reckoned quite accurately at 365.25, and the calendar provided for years of 365 days with an additional day in February every fourth year. In 46 B.C. a total of 90 days were intercalated into the year, bringing the calendar back into phase with the seasons. As a result, what would have been March 1, 45 B.C. was, in the new system, referred to as January 1, 45 B.C. Thus 46 B.C. was a long year, containing 445 days, and was referred to by Romans as *ultimus annus confusionis,* "the last year of the muddled reckoning."

In 10 B.C. it was found that the priests in charge of administering the new Roman calendar had wrongly intercalated the extra day every third year rather than every fourth. In order to rectify the situation, the emperor Augustus declared that no 366–day years should be observed for the next 12 years, and made certain that future intercalation would be properly conducted. With this minor adjustment, the Julian calendar was fully in place, so to remain for the next 1,626 years.

The Gregorian Calendar

Since the Julian calendar year of 365.25 days (averaging in the leap-year day) was slightly longer than the actual length of a solar year, 365.242199 days, over time even this system proved wanting, growing out of phase by about three or four days every four centuries. By the time of Pope Gregory XIII in the late sixteenth century, the difference between the calendar and the seasons had grown to ten days; the vernal equinox of 1582 occurred on March 11. Left without change, the Julian calendar would have resulted in fixed holy days occurring in the "wrong" season, which bewildered church officials. Moreover, certain fixed holy days were also used to determine when to plant and harvest crops.

Pope Gregory's reform, presented in the papal bull of February 24, 1582, consisted of deleting ten days from the year (the day following October 5 was designated as October 15) and declaring that three out of every four "century" years (1700, 1800, etc.) would not be leap years; if a century year, such as 1600, were divisible by 400, it would be a leap year. These modifications established the form of our present calendar.

In spite of its superior accuracy, the Gregorian calendar met with resistance in various parts of the world, and was not used until the eighteenth century in Protestant Europe and the American colonies, and even later still in areas under strong Byzantine influence.

Although the Gregorian calendar measures out a year that is slightly longer than the solar year (differing by about 25 seconds a year, or 3 days in every 10,000 years) its general workability and accuracy have led to its use worldwide for nearly all nonreligious purposes.

Calendar of Holidays

January

January 1
New Year's Day
Solemnity of Mary the Mother of God

January 1 or 2
St. Basil's Day

January 2
Second New Year

January 5–6
Epiphany Eve and Epiphany
Twelfth Night
Day of the Three Kings/Día de los Tres Reyes

First Monday after Twelfth Day
Plough Monday

January 6 or 7
Old Christmas

January 7
Gannā
St. Distaff's Day
St. John the Baptist's Day

January 11
St. Brictiva's Day

January 12
Old New Year's Day

January 12–15
Festival of Our Lord Bonfim

January 13
St. Knut's Day
Old Silvester

January 14
Magh Sankranti

January 15
Pilgrimage to the Shrine of the Black Christ
Adult's Day

January 16
St. Honoratus's Day

January 19 and 20
Timqat (Epiphany) and St. Michael's Feast

January 20
St. Sebastian's Day
St. Agnes Eve

January 21
St. Sarkis's Day

January 22
St. Dominique's Day (Midwife's Day)
St. Vincent's Day

January 24
Festival of Abundance

January 25
Burns Night

Last Tuesday in January
Up Helly Aa

Fifteenth Day, Shevat (January–February)
Tu Bi-Shevat (Fifteenth Day, Shevat)

Month of Magha (January–February)
Urn Festival

Month of Tagu, Days 1–4
Thingyan

Last Month, Last Day of Lunar Year
New Year's Eve

Moon 1, Days 1–15
New Year

Moon 1, Day 1
Tibetan New Year (Losar)

Moon 1, First Two Weeks (circa February)
Prayer Festival

Moon 1, Day 7
Festival of the Seven Grasses

Moon 1, Day 9
Making Happiness Festival

Moon 1, Days 14–19 (circa February)
Butter Sculpture Offering Festival

Moon 1, Day 15
Great Fifteenth
Burning of the Moon House Festival
Lantern Festival
Birthday of the Great Emperor–Official
of the Heavens

Moon 1, Day 16
Sixteenth Day

Moon 1, Day 19
Rats' Wedding Day

January–February
Rice Festival

Thai/Tai
Thai Poosam

February

Circa February
Tsagan Sara (New Year)

February
Clean Tent Ceremony
Winterlude

February 1
St. Brigid's Day

February 1–3 (circa)
Setsubun

February 2
Candlemas/Candelaria
Feast of the Virgin of the Suyapa
Queen of Waters Festival

February 3, 5
St. Blaise's Day, St. Agatha's Day

February 5
Igbi

February 10
Feast of St. Paul's Shipwreck

February 11
St. Vlasios's Day

February–March (Day 10 of Dhu'l-hija)
Id Al-Kabir (The Great Feast)

Moveable: February–March (Sunday before Lent)
Cheese Sunday

Moveable: February–March
Shrove Monday
Shrove Tuesday/Mardi Gras
Carnival
Ash Wednesday

Moveable: February–March (First Sunday in Lent)
Chalk Sunday

Moveable: February–April
Lent

February 14
St. Valentine's Day

Circa February 15–17
Igloo Festival

February 22
Boys' Day

February 25
St. George's Day

February 28
Feast of the Spring
Naked Festival

February 29
Leap Year Day/St. Oswald's Day

February (Full Moon)
Maka Buja

February–March (Full Moon)
Kason
Dol Purnima
Holi
Masi Magham

Pjalguna (February–March)
Sivaratri

Moon 2, Day 1 (February–March)
Wind Festival

February or March
Getting Out of the Water Festival (Kuomboko)

Moveable: February–March (Fourteenth Day of Adar)
Purim

March

First Two Weeks in March
Festival of the Water of Youth

March 1
First of March
St. David's Day

March 3
Hina Matsuri (Girls' Day)

Circa March 5
Feast of Excited Insects

March 8
Women's Day

March 9
Feast of the Forty Martyrs

Circa Mid-March, 1 Moons after Dosmoche
Storlog

March 17
St. Patrick's Day

March 19
St. Joseph's Day
Pookhyái

Circa March 20
Ibu Afo Festival
Emume Ala

Circa March 21
Vernal Equinox

Circa March 21 and Thirteen Days Thereafter
New Year

March 25
Day of the Annunciation

Moveable: March–April (Fourth Sunday in Lent)
Mothering Sunday

Moveable: March–April (Fifth Sunday in Lent)
Carlings Sunday

March–April (Saturday before Palm Sunday)
St. Lazarus's Day (Lazarovden)

March–April (Sunday before Easter)
Palm Sunday

Moveable: March 22–April 25
Easter and Holy Week

First Sunday after Easter (Low Sunday)

Domingo de Cuasimodo

St. Thomas's Day

Day after St. Thomas's Day (Low Sunday)

Blajini Day

Second Monday and Tuesday after Easter

Hocktide

Day 25 after Easter

Feast of Rousa

Day 28 after Easter

Ropotine

Moon 3, Day 5

Pure and Bright

Moon 3, Day 23

Birthday of Matsu

March–April

Gajan of Siva

Birthday of the Monkey God

Birthday of the Lord Vardhamana
Mahavira

March–April (Full Moon)

Panguni Uttiram

**Day 9, Bright Fortnight, Chaitra
(March–April)**

Ramanavami

March–May

Flying Fish Ceremony

April

Circa April

Road Building Festival

April

Awuru Odo

Cherry Blossom Festival

New Year

April 1

April Fools' Day

April 2

13 Farvardin/Sizdeh Bedar

April 4

St. Isidore's Day

April 5 or 6 (105 Days after the Winter Solstice)

Pure Brightness Festival

**Circa April (Eight Days Beginning on Day 15
of Nisan)**

Pesach/Passover

Last Day of Passover and Day after Passover

Maimona

April 12 or 13

New Year

April 13–15

New Year

April 19–25 (The Thursday in This Period)

First Day of Summer

April 23

St. George's Day

April 25

St. Mark's Day

April 30

May Eve

Walpurgis Night

Moon 4, Day 8

Buddha's Birthday

April (Various Dates)

Planting Festivals

Wangkang Festival

April–May

First of Baisakh/Vaisakh

**Full Moon (Purnima) of Vaisakha
(April–May)**

Buddha Jayanti

May

Circa May (Day 33 of the Omer Period)
Lag Ba-omer

May
Nongkrem Dance

May (Throughout the Month)
Flowers of May

First Sunday in May
Sunday School Day

First Tuesday in May
Fool's Fair

May 1
May Day
St. Joseph's Day

May 1–May 30
Birth of the Buffalo God

May 3
Day of the Holy Cross

May 5
Cinco de Mayo

May 5 (Formerly Moon 5, Day 5)
Boys' Day

Easter to July
Holy Ghost Season

Monday, Tuesday, and Wednesday before Ascension
Rogation Days

Moveable: Forty Days after Easter
Ascension Day

Moveable: Fifty Days after Easter
Whitsun/Pentecost

First Sunday after Whitsunday
Trinity

Moveable: Thursday after Trinity
Corpus Christi/Body of Christ

Seventh Thursday after Easter
Semik

First Thursday after Corpus Christi
Lajkonik

May 11–14
Ice Saints

May 14
Crossmas

May 15
St. Sofia's Day
St. Isidore's Day

May 17
Death of the Ground

May 24
Queen's Bithday (Victoria Day)

May 24–25
Pilgrimage of Sainte Sara

May 25
St. Urban's Day

May 29
Oak-Apple Day (Royal Oak Day)

May 31
Memorial Day (Day of the Dead)

May (Full Moon)
Wesak Day

Moon 5, Day 5 (May–June)
Double Fifth
Tano

Moon 5, Day 14
Gods of the Sea Festival (and Boat Race Day)

Moon 5, Day 15
Gogatsumatsuri

May–June
Sithinakha/Kumar Sasthi
Vata Savitri
Rocket Festival

May–June (Jaistha)
Ganga Dussehra

May–June (Day 6 of Sivan)
Shavuot

May to July (Height of Rainy Season)
Okere Juju

Circa May–July
Days 1–10 of Muharram

Late May or Early June
Star Snow (Qoyllur Rit'i)

June

Early June
Tyas Tuyï

June
Egungun Festival

June 1–2
Gawai Dayak

June 11
Cataclysmos Day

June 13
St. Anthony's Day

June 13–29
Festas Juninas

June 22–August 21
Aobao Gathering

June 24
St. John's Day/Midsumer Day
Day of the Indian

June 25
Festival of the Plow

June 27–July 27
Lesser New Year

June 29
Day of St. Peter and St. Paul

June or July (Rainy Season)
Car Festival (Rath Jatra)

Moon 8, Waning Day–Moon 11, Full Moon (June/July to September/October)
Vossa/Khao Vatsa/Waso

Moon 6, Day 6
Airing the Classics

Moon 6, Day 15
Shampoo Day (Yoodoonal)

Moon 6, Day 24
Birthday of the Lotus
Yi (China) New Year

May to October, Peaking in July
Festa Season

June–July or August–September
Pola and Hadaga

Late June to Early September
Powwow

July

Circa July
Olojo Festival (Ogun Festival)

Early July
Festival of the Ears of Grain

July
Nazareth Baptist Church Festival

July 1–2
Canada Day/Dominion Day

July 2 and August 16
Palio

July 4
Independence Day/Fourth of July

July 6
Feast of San Fermin

July 8
Feast of St. Elizabeth

July 11
Naadam Festival

July 14
   Bastille Day

July 15
   St. Swithin's Day
   Festival of the Virgin of Carmen

July 25
   St. James's Day

July 26
   St. Anne's Day
   Pardon of Ste. Ann d'Auray

July 29
   St. Olaf's Wake

Moon 7, Day 7 (July–August)
   Birthday of the Seven Old Maids
   Star Festival/Double Seventh

Moon 7, Days 13–15 (July–August)
   Obon

Moon 7, Day 15 (July–August)
   Hungry Ghost Festival

July–August
   Procession of Sacred Cows
   Ghanta Karna
   Kandy Esala Perahera
   Marya
   Snake Festival
   Teej
   Tish-Ah Be-Av

July–August (Full Moon)
   Sacred Thread Festival

July or August
   Maggomboh
   Imechi Festival

Late July–First Tuesday of August
   Carnival

Late July or Early August
   Carnival

Full Moon in Summer
   Tea Meetings

August

Early August
   Llama Festival

August
   Good Year Festival
   Panchadaan

August 1
   Feast of the Progress of the Precious
      and Vivifying Cross
   Honey Day
   Lammas
   Lúghnasa
   Parents Day

August 2
   Feast Day of Our Lady of the Angeles

August 2–7
   Nebuta Festival

August 6
   Transfiguration of Christ

August 10
   Festival of St. Laurence

August 10–12
   Puck's Fair

August 15
   Assumption of the Virgin

August 20
   St. Stephen's Fete

Circa August 24
   Thanksgiving

August 30
   La Rose

End of August
   Reed Dance

August–September
   Prachum Ben
   Feast of the Dead
   Festival of the Elephant God
   Gokarna Aunsi

Plough Festival
Janmashtami
Lord Krishna's Birthday
Khordad-Sal
Paryushana
Agwunsi Festival
Insect-Hearing Festival

Moon 8, Day 15 (August–September)
Mid-Autumn Feast

Moon 8, Day 16 (August–September)
Birthday of the Monkey God

Various Dates
Harvest Festivals

September

Circa September
Okpesi Festival

September
Indra Jatra

September 8
Nativity of the Virgin

First and Second Days of Tishri (September–October)
Rosh Hashana

September 11
Coptic New Year
Enkutatash (New Year)

September 14
Holy Cross Day

September 15
Keiro no Hi (Respect for the Elderly Day)

Tenth Day of Tishri
Yom Kippur

12 Rabi-ul Awal (August–October)
Ma-ulid

Circa September 21–22
Autumnal Equinox
Jūgowa

September 27
Maskal

September 29
St. Michael's Day

Fifth Day of the Fifth Lunar Month (Late September–Early October)
Bon Kate

Moon 9, Day 9 (September–October)
Double Ninth
Chrysanthemum Day
Festival of the Nine Imperial Gods

Month 10 (September–October)
Ho Khao Slak

Days 24 and 25 of Tishri (September–October)
Simhat Torah and Is'ru Chag

September–October
Durga Puja/Dasain/Dussehra/Durgotsava
Oktoberfest
Pitra Visarjana Amavasya

October

Circa October (Wagyut Moon, Day 15)
Ok Pansa/Ok Vatsa/Thadingyut

October
Lord of the Earthquake

First Sunday in October
St. Michael's Day
Water Festival

Second Sunday in October
Lotu-A-Tamaiti

October 5
Han'gul Day

October 7
Festival of the Virgin of Rosario

October 17
Romería of Our Lady of Valme

October 18
St. Luke's Day

October 21
Festival of the Black Christ

October 25
St. Crispin and St. Crispinian's Day

October 26
St. Demetrius's Day

October 28
Thanksgiving
Punkie Night

October 31
All Hallow's Eve/All Saints' Eve

Moon 10, Day 1 (October–November)
Sending the Winter Dress

Moon 10, Day 25 (October–November)
Sang-joe

Kartik (October–November)
Gopashtami ("Cow Eighth") and
Govardhan Puja

October–November
Diwali/Deepavali/Tihar
Karwachoth

**Seven Days, Beginning Fifteenth of Tishri
(October–November)**
Sukkot

**Moveable: October or Later (after Rainy
Season)**
Mother's Day

November

Late Autumn
Keretkun Festival

Circa November
Seal Festival
Loi Krathong

Early November (Near End of Rainy Season)
Sango Festival

November
Tori-no-inchi

November 1
All Saints' Day

November 2
All Souls' Day

Friday before November 3
Creole Day

November 3
St. Hubert's Day

November 5
Guy Fawkes Night

**Twenty-seventh Day of Rajab (November 6
in 1999)**
Night of the Ascension

November 8
St. Michael's Day

November 11
St. Martin's Day
St. Mennas's Day

November 15
Shichi-go-san (Seven-Five-Three)

Circa November 15
Haile Selassie's Coronation Day

November 18
Feast of St. Plato the Martyr

November 19
Settlement Day

November 21
Presentation of the Virgin Mary in the
Temple

November 25
St. Catherine's Day

Fourth Thursday in November
Thanksgiving

November 30
St. Andrew's Day

Moon 8, Day 29 (November)
Seged

Month 12 (November)
Boun Phan Vet

Moveable: Month of Shaban
Shaban

Moveable: November–December
Ramadan (Month of Fasting)

December

Circa December (Tasaungmon Full Moon)
Tawadeintha/Tazaungdaing

Sunday before Advent (Early December)
Stir-Up Sunday

Four Weeks before Christmas, Beginning on a Sunday
Advent Season

Early December (Variable)
Bear Festival

Circa December (Eight Days Beginning on 25 Kislev)
Hanukkah

December 4
St. Barbara's Day

December 6
St. Nicholas's Day

December 7
Burning the Devil

Circa December 7–8
Itul

December 8
Immaculate Conception
Needle Day

Second Sunday before Christmas
Mother's Day

December 12
Our Lady of Guadalupe

December 13
St. Lucy's Day

December 14
St. Spiridion Day

December 16
Braaiveleis

December 16–25
Cock Crow Mass

Sunday before Christmas
Father's Day

Friday before Christmas
Cuci Negeri

December 18
St. Modesto's Day

Circa December 21
Ysyakh

December 21
St. Thomas's Day

Circa December 22
Winter Solstice

December 23
Festival of St. Naum
St. Thorlak's Day
La Noche de Rabanos (Night of the Radishes)

December 25–30 (Variable)
Kushi Festival

December 25
Christmas

December 26
Boxing Day
Kwanzaa
St. Stephen's Day

December 27
St. John's Day

December 28
Holy Innocents' Day

December 31
New Year's Eve
Sylvester Day

Late December
Sing-Sing

Moon 12, Day 8 (December–January)
Rice Cake Festival

Moon 12, Day 20 (December–January)
Day for Sweeping Floors

Moon 12, Day 23 or 24 (December–January)
Kitchen God Visits Heaven

Moon 12, Day 28 (December–January)
King's New Year

December–January
Little Feast

December–August
Odo

Words to Know

A

Absolute monarchy: A form of government in which a king or queen has absolute control over the people, who have no voice in their government.

Act of merit: An act of charity that, in Buddhism, is said to help the doer find favor with Buddha and earn credits toward a good rebirth.

Advent: A Christian holiday. From the Latin *adventus*, "coming," referring to the birth of Jesus. Advent is a four-week period of preparation for Christmas, beginning on the Sunday nearest November 30.

Age of Enlightenment: A philosophical movement during the eighteenth century when European writers, journalists, and philosophers influenced thousands through new ideas about an individual's right to determine his or her own destiny in life, including having a voice in government. The movement emphasized the use of reason to challenge previously accepted church teachings and traditions and thus is sometimes referred to as the Age of Reason.

Aliyah: From the Hebrew for "ascent" or "going up." The waves of Jewish immigrants to Israel in the nineteenth and twentieth centuries.

Allah: The "one God" of Islam.

Ancestors: A person's, tribe's, or cultural group's forefathers or recently deceased relatives.

Asceticism: A way of life marked by severe self-denial as a form of personal and spiritual discipline; for example, depriving the body of food and owning few material goods.

Ash Wednesday: A Christian holiday. Ash Wednesday is the seventh Wednesday before Easter and the first day of Lent, a season of fasting commemorating Jesus Christ's forty days of temptation in the wilderness. The name is derived from the practice of priests placing ashes on the foreheads of worshipers as a remembrance "that you are dust and unto dust you shall return."

B

Bastille: A castle and fortress in Paris, France, built in 1370 and later used as a prison. Bastille Day commemorates the storming of the Bastille by French peasants and workers on July 14, 1789, sparking the French Revolution.

Bee: A large gathering, usually of farm families, to complete a task and celebrate with food and drink, games, and dancing.

Beignet: A square fritter without a hole that is a popular snack during Carnival in France and French-influenced New Orleans, Louisiana. Fried pastries are popular throughout the world during Carnival, a time when people traditionally tried to use up their butter and animal fat before the Christian holiday of Lent.

Black Madonna: Poland's most famous religious icon, a painting of the Virgin Mary holding the infant Jesus, said to have been painted by Saint Luke during the first century A.D.

Blessing baskets: Baskets of Easter foods and pysanky (Easter eggs), covered with hand-embroidered cloths and carried to church to be blessed on Holy Saturday in Ukraine and Poland.

Bodhi tree: The "tree of wisdom." Buddha achieved enlightenment while sitting under a bodhi tree.

Bourgeoisie: In French, the middle social class.

Buddha: Prince Siddhartha Gautama (c. 563–c. 483 B.C.) of India, later given the name Buddha ("the Enlightened One"). His teachings became the foundation of Buddhism.

Buddhism: One of the major religions of Asia and one of the five largest religious systems in the world. Buddhists believe that suffering is an inescapable part of life and that peace can be achieved only by practicing charity, temperance, justice, honesty, and truth. They also believe in a continual cycle of birth, illness, death, and rebirth.

Byzantine Empire: The Eastern Roman Empire, with its capital at Constantinople (present-day Istanbul, Turkey).

C

Cajun: The name given to French Canadians who emigrated from Acadia, a former name for Nova Scotia. The name was eventually shortened from "Acadian" to "Cajun."

Calligraphy: Ornamental handwriting. In Islam, it is the Arabic script in which the Koran is written and which is used inside mosques as an art form.

Calypso: A popular musical style originating in Trinidad and Tobago in which singers create witty lyrics to a particular rhythm.

Carnavalesco: An individual who helps design, plan, and choreograph Carnival parades and shows in Brazil.

Caste system: A social system in which people are divided into classes according to their skin color and ancestry.

Catholic Church: The ancient undivided Christian church or a church claiming historical continuity from it.

Celts: A people who lived in Ireland, Scotland, England, Wales, and northern France before the birth of Christ, more than two thousand years ago. Also refers to modern people of these areas.

Chinese zodiac: A zodiac system based on a twelve-year cycle, with each year named after one of twelve animals. A person's zodiac sign is the animal representing the year in which he or she was born.

Christian Protestantism: Christian church denominations that reject certain aspects of Catholicism and Orthodox Christianity and believe in salvation by faith alone, the Holy Bible as the only source of God's revealed truth, and the "priesthood" of all believers.

Civil disobedience: Nonviolent action, such as protest marches, taken by an individual or group in an attempt to bring about social change.

Civil rights: Rights granted to every member of a society regardless of race, sex, age, creed, or religious beliefs. Specifically, the rights given by certain amendments to the U.S. Constitution.

Collective farm: A large farm, especially in former communist countries, formed by combining many small farms for joint operation under government control.

Colonial rule: A country's rule of a foreign land that has settlers from the ruling country, or colonists, living there.

Commedia dell'arte: Italian comedy of the sixteenth to eighteenth centuries that created some of the most famous characters in Italian costume. Among them are Harlequin, with his multicolored suit, and Punchinello, who later became a famous character in puppet shows.

Communism: A political and economic system in which the government controls and owns the means of production of goods and distributes the goods equally among the population.

Concentration camps: Nazi German military camps where civilians, primarily Jews, were held during World War II (1939–45). Millions were tortured, gassed, or burned to death in these camps.

Constitutional monarchy: A form of government in which a nation is ruled by a king or queen but the people are represented through executive, legislative, and judicial branches.

Continental Congress: Men representing twelve of the thirteen American colonies (all but Georgia) who formed a colonial government in 1774 in Philadelphia, Pennsylvania, and set forth the principles of the American Revolution (1775–83).

Cornucopia: A horn-shaped basket overflowing with vegetables and fruits. The cornucopia is a symbol of a bountiful harvest, often used as a Thanksgiving decoration. Also called "horn of plenty."

Council of Nicaea: In 325, a church governing body led by Roman emperor Constantine (reigned 306–37) met in the city of Nicaea (in what is now Turkey). The council formally established the Feast of Christ's Resurrection (Easter) and decreed that it should be celebrated on the Sunday following the first full moon after the spring equinox.

Coup d'état: A military takeover of an existing government.

Crazy days: In many European countries, the final days of Carnival celebrations, the wildest and most widely celebrated.

Creole: A person descended from or culturally related to early French or sometimes Spanish settlers of the U.S. Gulf Coast; they preserve a characteristic form of French speech and culture.

Crucifixion: A Roman method of execution, in which a person is nailed to a wooden cross to die.

Crusades: Religious wars of the eleventh, twelfth, and thirteenth centuries in which Christians fought to win the Holy Land from the Muslims.

D

Dedication: The setting apart of a temple or church for sacred uses with solemn rites.

Dharma: Laws of nature that were taught by Buddha. The primary symbol of Buddhism is a wheel with eight spokes, called the dharma wheel, which symbolizes life's constant cycles of change and the Eightfold Path to enlightenment.

Diaspora: The breaking up and scattering of a people from their homeland, especially the scattering of the Jewish people from Israel throughout the world.

Divination: Predicting the future through ritual; fortune-telling.

Dragon parade: A Chinese New Year parade featuring long dragon costumes manipulated by many dancers.

Dreidel: A four-sided top, each side marked with a Hebrew letter, all together representing the phrase "A great miracle happened there," referring to the Hanukkah miracle in ancient Jerusalem. The term also refers to the Hanukkah game played by Jewish children with the top.

Druids: An order of Celtic priests.

E

Easter bunny: Originally the Easter hare, called "Oschter Haws" by the Germans; a mythical rabbit who is said to bring colored eggs and candy to children on Easter Sunday.

Easter egg: An egg colored or decorated for Easter.

Easter lily: The white trumpet lily, native to Bermuda but widely cultivated in the United States. It blooms at Easter time and is known as a symbol of purity and of Christ's Resurrection.

Eastern Orthodox Church: A branch of the Christian church with many members in Eastern Europe, Western Asia, and the Mediterranean. The Eastern Orthodox Church began in the Greek city of Constantinople (now Istanbul, Turkey), the seat of

Roman emperor Constantine's (reigned 306–37) Eastern Roman Empire.

Elders: Older family or community members, such as grandparents, who are honored and respected for their experience and wisdom.

Enlightenment: Understanding the truth about human existence; a spiritual state marked by the absence of desire or suffering, upon which Buddhist teaching is based.

Epiphany of Our Lord: A Christian holiday. Traditionally observed on January 6, Epiphany marks the official end of the Christmas season. In Western Christian churches, Epiphany commemorates the visit of the Three Wise Men to see the infant Jesus in Bethlehem; in Eastern Orthodox churches, it is celebrated as the day of Jesus' baptism.

Epitaphion: A carved structure covered with a gold-embroidered cloth and decorated with flowers that is a symbol of Christ's tomb in the Greek Orthodox Church.

Epitaphios: "Feast of Sorrow." A Good Friday ritual in the Greek Orthodox Church, enacted as a funeral procession for Jesus Christ.

Equinox: The first day of spring and the first day of fall of each year, when the length of the day's sunlight is equal to the length of the day's darkness. This occurs on about March 20 or 21 and September 22 or 23.

Essence: The "spirit" of a thing, such as food or burnt offerings, which is believed to be usable by the dead in many cultures.

F

Fantasia: "Fantasy." Brazilian name for Carnival costume.

Fast: To voluntarily go without food or drink, often as part of religious practice, as during Ramadan or Lent.

Feudal system: The predominant economic and social structure in Europe from about the ninth to the fifteenth centuries, in which peasants farmed land for nobles and in turn received a small house and plot of land for themselves.

First fruits: The first harvesting of a crop, considered sacred by many cultures.

Folk holiday: A nonreligious holiday that originates with the common people.

Fool societies: In Germany and other parts of Europe, guilds formed by tradesmen to plan and organize Carnival celebrations.

Four Noble Truths: The four principles that became the core of Buddha's teaching: 1) Suffering is everywhere; 2) The cause of suffering is the attempt to satisfy selfish desires; 3) Suffering can be stopped by overcoming selfish desires; and 4) The way to end craving and suffering is to follow the Eightfold Path, eight steps concerning the right way to think and conduct oneself.

Freedom of the press: The right of people to publish and distribute pamphlets, newspapers, and journals containing their own thoughts and observations without censorship by government or church.

French Quarter: A historical section of New Orleans, Louisiana, where the wildest and most elaborate Mardi Gras celebrations are staged.

G

Gelt: The traditional Jewish name for money given to the poor during Hanukkah. Also refers to any Hanukkah gift and to play money (chocolate coins wrapped in gold foil) used in playing dreidel.

Gilles: A special men's society in Belgium whose members dress in identical costumes and masks and march in Mardi Gras parades.

Golden Stool of the Ashanti: A wooden stool covered with a layer of gold. The stool is sacred to the Ashanti people of Ghana, to whom it is a symbol of their nation and their king.

Good Friday: The Friday before Easter Sunday, a day for mourning Christ's death.

Gregorian calendar: The calendar in general use in much of the world in modern times. It was introduced by Pope Gregory XIII in 1582 as a modification of the Roman Julian calendar.

Griot: A storyteller who passes on the history of a people orally and through music.

Guerrilla: A member of a small military organization that uses unconventional fighting tactics to surprise and ambush their enemies.

Guillotine: A machine for beheading criminals, widely used by French revolutionaries during the late 1700s and for many years afterward in France. It consisted of a wooden frame with a heavy, tapered blade hoisted to the top and then dropped, immediately severing the victim's head.

Guising: An old Scottish custom of dressing in disguise and going from house to house asking for treats; a forerunner of Halloween trick-or-treating.

H

Hanukkiah: A Hanukkah menorah, or candleholder. It has eight main branches and a ninth for the servant candle, used to light the other eight.

Harvest festival: A festival for celebrating the gathering of crops at the end of the growing season.

Harvest moon: The full moon nearest to the time of the fall equinox (about September 23), so called because it occurs at the traditional time of harvest in the Northern Hemisphere. It appears larger and brighter than the usual full moon, and the moon is full for an extra night, giving farmers more hours to harvest crops.

Hegira: The flight of Muhammad and his followers in 622 from Mecca to Yathrib, later known as Medina, where Muhammad was accepted as a prophet. The Hegira marks the beginning of the Islamic calendar.

Hidalgo's bell: A cathedral bell rung by Father Miguel Hidalgo y Costilla in the town of Dolores on September 16, 1810, to call the native people of Mexico together in a revolt against Spanish rule.

Hinduism: The major religion of India and one of the world's oldest religions. It is based on the natural laws of dharma and conforming to one's duty through ritual, social observances, and meditation.

Holocaust: The mass slaughter by the Nazis of some six million Jews and thousands of other European civilians during World War II (1939–45), chiefly by gassing and burning the victims.

Holy Communion: A church rite in which Christians eat and drink blessed bread and wine as memorials of Christ's death. Christ is said to have initiated the rite during the Last Supper.

Holy Grail: A cup or plate that, according to medieval legend, Jesus used at the Last Supper.

Holy Land: Palestine, where Jesus Christ lived, preached, died, and was resurrected, according to the Bible. Major holy sites are Jerusalem and Bethlehem.

Holy Shroud: In the Orthodox Church in Ukraine, a specially woven and embroidered cloth that represents Jesus' burial cloth, used for Holy Week services.

I

Icons: Religious scenes or figures such as Christ and the Virgin Mary, usually very old, painted on wooden panels or on linen or cotton cloth glued to panels. Revered by Christians in the Eastern Orthodox and Catholic Churches, some are believed to have miraculous powers.

Iftar: The nighttime feast served after sunset during Ramadan.

Imam: Person who leads prayer and recites from the Koran during worship services in a mosque.

Immigrants: People who leave their home country and enter another to settle.

Islam: The major religion of the Middle East, northern Africa, parts of Southeast Asia, and some former Soviet Union countries. Islam is the world's second-largest religion. Believers, called Muslims, worship their one god, Allah, and assert that Muhammad (c. 570–632), founder of Islam, is his prophet.

Islamic calendar: The lunar calendar used to determine the date of Islamic holidays. Each of twelve months begins with the first sighting of the new moon. Each lunar month has either twenty-nine or thirty days, and each year has 354 days.

J

Jataka Tales: A collection of more than five-hundred tales said to have been told by Buddha. The tales were passed down orally through generations and finally written down several hundred years after his death. About Buddha's previous lives, the tales concern such issues as responsibility, friendship, honesty, ecology, and respect for elders.

Jesus Christ: The founder of Christianity. Jesus was born in Bethlehem in about 6 B.C. and died in about A.D. 30, when he was crucified. According to Christian tradition,

Jesus was the Son of God, and he came into the world to die for the sins of mankind. His followers believe that as Christ rose from the dead and ascended into heaven, so too will they.

Julian calendar: The calendar introduced in Rome in 46 B.C. and on which the modern-day Gregorian calendar is based.

K

Kitchen God: A Chinese deity honored during the lunar New Year. He is said to reside in the kitchen and report to the Jade Emperor (the highest deity, who resides in heaven) once a year on the actions of each household.

Koran: The Islamic holy book, written in Arabic and containing Scriptures also found in the Jewish Torah and the Christian Bible, as well as rules on all aspects of human living. The Koran is believed to have been revealed to the prophet Muhammad by Allah through the angel Gabriel.

Krewes: Secretive, members-only clubs that organize Mardi Gras parades and activities in New Orleans, Louisiana.

L

Lakshmi: The Hindu goddess of wealth, honored during Diwali, the Hindu New Year.

Last Supper: Also called the Lord's Supper; the last meal Jesus Christ shared with his disciples, believed to have been a Passover

meal and at which Christ is said to have initiated the rite of Holy Communion. Christians observe the Thursday before Easter in memory of the Last Supper.

Legal holiday: A day declared an official holiday by a government, meaning that government offices, schools, and usually banks and other offices are closed so that workers may observe the holiday.

Lent: A Christian holiday. Lent is the traditional six-week period of partial fasting that precedes Easter. It is a time to remember the forty days that Jesus wandered in the desert without food. Many Christians give up a favorite food or activity during Lent.

Lunar New Year: A movable holiday marking the first day of the first lunar month on the Chinese lunar calendar. It begins at sunset on the day of the second new moon following the winter solstice (between late January and the end of February) and ends on the fifteenth day of the first lunar month.

M

Mardi Gras: *See* Shrove Tuesday.

Martyr: One who voluntarily suffers death for proclaiming his or her religious beliefs and refusing to give them up.

Masked ball: A formal dance at which those attending wear costumes and masks that conceal their identity.

Mass: A celebration of the Christian sacrament of the Eucharist (Holy Communion), commemorating the sacrifice of the body and blood of Christ, symbolized by consecrated bread and wine.

Maundy Thursday: The Thursday before Easter Sunday, said to be the day Christ took the Last Supper, prayed in the Garden of Gethsemane, was betrayed by Judas Iscariot, and was arrested. In many churches, this is a day for taking Holy Communion in memory of the Last Supper.

Mecca: The holiest city of Islam. It is located in Saudi Arabia and is the birthplace of the prophet Muhammad. Muslims strive to make a pilgrimage to Mecca at least once during their lifetime and face toward Mecca each time they pray.

Menorah: A seven-pronged candleholder used in Jewish worship ceremonies.

Messiah: The "anointed," the Savior prophesied in the Bible to save the world from sin. To Christians, the Messiah is Jesus Christ.

Metta: One of Buddha's main teachings, involving the concept of loving kindness. Metta is a way to overcome anger through love, evil through good, and untruth through truth.

Middle Path: A major tenant of Buddhism advocating equilibrium (balance) between extremes in life and avoiding things or ideas produced by selfish desires. Buddhists believe the best way to travel the Middle Path is through meditation, as Buddha did.

Mishnah: The Jewish code of law, passed down orally for centuries before being written down by rabbis during the second century.

Missionaries: People sent to other countries to teach their religious beliefs to native peoples and carry on humanitarian work.

Monk: A man who is a member of a religious order and usually lives in a monastery or wanders from place to place teaching religious principles.

Monsoon: The name give to a season of heavy rains and wind in India and southern Asia.

Mosque: An Islamic temple for prayer and worship, consisting of a large dome and at least one pointed tower, or minaret. Mosques are decorated with calligraphy from the Koran.

Movable holiday: A holiday that falls at a different time each year, depending on the calendar used to determine the celebration. For example, Thanksgiving, Ramadan, and Easter.

Muhammad: Islam's greatest prophet. Muhammad was an Arabian who lived during the sixth century (c. 570–632). He is considered the founder of Islam.

Mumming: Merrymaking in disguise during festivals.

Muslim: A follower of the Islamic faith.

N

Nativity: The birth of Jesus Christ, as told in the biblical New Testament.

Nazarenos: Honorable men who lead Holy Week processions in Spain, wearing long robes and pointed hoods that cover their faces.

New moon: The thin crescent moon that appears after sunset following nights during the beginning of the new moon phase, when no moon can be seen. The new moon is used to mark the beginning of each month in both the Islamic and Jewish calendars.

Night of Power: The twenty-seventh night of Ramadan, which Muslims believe is the night when the angel Gabriel first began giving the words of the Koran to the prophet Muhammad.

Nirvana: A state of perfect peace and joy; freedom from greed, anger, and sorrow.

Nun: A woman who is a member of a religious order.

O

Ofrenda: Spanish word for an offering made to the dead or to a religious figure.

Oratorio: A long choral music piece for many voices, without action or scenery, usually on a religious theme. For example, Handel's *Messiah.*

P

Pagan: Referring to the worship of many gods, especially to early peoples who worshiped gods of nature.

Palm Sunday: The Sunday before Easter, when Jesus' entry into Jerusalem is com-

memorated with palms, which were used to line his path.

Papier-mâché: A mixture of flour, paper, paste, and water that hardens when dry and is often used to create figures and objects for Carnival parade floats and for many other craft projects.

Parade float: A large platform that is elaborately decorated and carries people and scenery representing a specific parade theme. Floats are usually mounted on a trailer and pulled through the streets by a motor vehicle. Float design and building is often considered an art.

Parol: A traditional Filipino symbol of Christmas, a star-shaped lantern made from bamboo and paper, called the Star of Bethlehem.

Paschal candle: A large candle, sometimes weighing hundreds of pounds, that is lit in some churches on Holy Saturday and used to light many individual candles for congregation members. The Paschal candle represents Christ as the light of the world.

Passion of Jesus Christ: The sufferings that Christ endured between the night of the Last Supper with his disciples and his death by crucifixion, often reenacted by Christians during Holy Week.

Passion play: A dramatic musical play reenacting Christ's Passion and crucifixion.

Passover: An observance of the Jews' deliverance from slavery in Egypt, as told in the Bible. Jewish families were commanded to smear the blood of a sacrificial lamb on their doorways so that the angel of death would pass over their homes. Passover is still a major Jewish observance. Christians also commemorate Passover by taking Holy Communion on Maundy Thursday, the day Christ is said to have eaten a Passover meal with his disciples at the Last Supper.

Patron saint: A saint believed to represent and protect a group of people, church, nation, city or town, animals, or objects. A saint to whom people pray for help in certain circumstances.

Penitents: In Holy Week processions in Spain, the Philippines, and Central and South America, persons who walk in the procession carrying heavy wooden crosses, in chains, or whipping themselves as punishment and repentance for wrongs they have done and to commemorate Christ's suffering as he carried the Cross.

Pilgrimage: A journey, usually to a holy place or shrine.

Pilgrims: Name given to English colonists who arrived at what is now Plymouth, Massachusetts, in 1621 and settled there. This group is credited with celebrating the first Thanksgiving, with members of the Wampanoag Indian tribe.

Pongol: A sweet, boiled rice dish that is prepared to celebrate the rice harvest in parts of India. Pongol is also the name given to this holiday.

Pope: A high-ranking bishop who is head of the Roman Catholic Church and resides in the Vatican in Rome.

Proclamation: An official formal public announcement, usually by a government leader or representative.

Promised Land: According to the biblical book of Genesis, the land of Canaan, promised by God to Abraham, the father of the Jews. The prophet Moses led the Hebrews to the Promised Land after freeing them from slavery in Egypt. Refers to modern-day Israel.

Prophet: One who speaks for God or a deity; a divinely inspired speaker, interpreter, or spokesperson who passes on to the people things revealed to him or her by God.

Proverb: A wise saying or adage, often part of the cultural heritage of a people.

Puritans: Members of a sixteenth- and seventeenth-century religious Protestant group in England and New England that believed in a strict work ethic and opposed ceremony and celebration.

Pysanky: Ukrainian and Polish Easter eggs created by using the wax resist, or batik, method.

R

Rabbi: A Jewish religious teacher and leader.

Reincarnation: A Hindu belief that all life is part of a universal creative force called Brahman and that human and animal souls are reborn into new bodies many times before they return to Brahman.

Resurrection of Jesus Christ: The rising from the dead of Jesus Christ, the central figure of Christianity, worshiped as the son of God. The Resurrection is celebrated at Easter. Christians believe that Christ died to reconcile humans with God and that believers will have eternal life of the spirit.

S

Sabzeh: A dish of sprouts grown by Iranian families in preparation for Nouruz, the New Year celebration. The sprouts are said to absorb bad luck from the past year.

Saint: A person, usually deceased, who has been officially recognized by church officials as holy because of deeds performed during his or her lifetime.

Samba: A fast dance made famous in Rio de Janeiro, Brazil, in which the feet and hips move but the upper body is kept still. The samba is performed by large groups of dancers, called samba schools, who wear elaborate matching costumes in Carnival parades.

Samhain: An annual festival of the Celts that marked the end of the fall harvest and the beginning of winter. It is said to be the forerunner of Halloween and New Year celebrations in parts of Europe.

Sangha: A Buddhist community of monks and nuns.

Secular: Nonreligious.

Seven Principles of Kwanzaa: A set of principles developed for Kwanzaa laying out rules of living for the community of people of African descent: unity, self-determination, collective work and responsibility, cooperative economics, purpose, creativity, and faith.

Shofar: An ancient Jewish traditional trumpet-like instrument made from a ram's or antelope's horn that is blown in the synagogue during Rosh Hashanah and Yom Kippur.

Shrine: A place, either natural or manmade, set aside for worship of a god or saint; a box or structure containing religious relics or images.

Shrove Tuesday: The Tuesday before Ash Wednesday, also called Fat Tuesday (Mardi Gras in French). Shrove Tuesday is the final day of Carnival and the one on which the biggest celebrations are held. Traditionally a time for confessing sins (called "being shriven") and for using up the fresh meat and animal fat, eggs, and butter in the household before the forty-day fast of Lent.

Solstice: The first day of summer and the first day of winter in the northern hemisphere, when daylight hours are the longest and shortest, respectively. The solstices fall about June 22 and December 22 of each year.

Spring couplets: Two-line rhymes written in Chinese calligraphy that are displayed during Chinese New Year as a wish for good luck.

Star of David: A six-pointed star believed to have decorated the shield of King David of Israel, who ruled about 1000 B.C. A widely used symbol of Judaism.

Stations of the Cross: The locations in Jerusalem and the corresponding events leading to the Crucifixion and Resurrection of Christ. A central theme of Christian religious art and sculpture, Holy Week processions, and Passion plays.

Steel drum: A drum created in Trinidad and Tobago, originally by using discarded steel oil barrels. Steel drum bands and music have become popular worldwide.

Suhur: The pre-dawn meal served each morning of Ramadan.

Supernatural: Transcending the laws of nature; referring to ghosts and spirits and the spiritual realm.

Superstition: A belief that something will happen or not happen as a result of performing a specific ritual, for example, eating certain foods to bring good luck.

Swahili: A major African language. Many of the terms relating to Kwanzaa are drawn from Swahili.

Synagogue: A Jewish house of worship.

T

Tableau: A group of people in costume creating a living picture or scene portraying a historical, mythological, musical, or narrative theme.

Taboo: Something forbidden by religious or cultural rules, sometimes because of the fear of punishment by supernatural powers.

Talmud: The authoritative book of Jewish tradition, consisting of the Mishnah and the Gemara, comments of rabbis about the Mishnah.

Tamboradas: Loud, steady drumbeats that sound in many Spanish cities and villages beginning at midnight on Holy Thursday and continuing until late on Holy Saturday night, announcing the Passion and death of Christ.

Throws: Objects such as plastic bead necklaces and coins, flowers, candy, or fruit thrown to the crowd from parade floats or by marching groups, especially in Carnival parades.

Torah: The Jewish holy book, consisting of the five books of Moses (first five books of the biblical Old Testament), also called the Pentateuch.

Trick-or-treating: A widely popular Halloween tradition for children in which they dress in costumes and go from door to door collecting candy and treats. Children once played tricks on those who did not give treats.

V

Vaya: A sprig of bay or myrtle attached to a small cross made from a palm frond, given by Greek Orthodox priests to members of their congregation on Palm Sunday.

Vegetarian: Eating no meat, and sometimes no animal products, such as dairy foods or eggs.

Viceroy: The governor of a country or territory who rules in the name of a king or queen.

Virgin of Guadalupe: The Virgin Mary, mother of Jesus Christ, as she is said to have appeared (with dark skin and Mexican Indian clothing) to an Indian woodcutter in 1531. She is the patron saint of Mexico's poor.

W

Witch: A woman accused of worshiping Satan and casting spells to help him do evil to humans. Witches are often fictitious characters and the subject of Halloween costumes.

Y

Yule log: A large log burned in a fireplace during the Christmas season, a custom that began in early Europe and Scandinavia.

Z

Zakat: Money given by Muslims to help the poor in obedience to the laws of Islam and as a means of worshiping Allah.

Zion: The name of a fortification in the ancient city of Jerusalem, capital of King David's kingdom in about 1000 B.C. For centuries, Zion has been a symbol of the Promised Land (Israel) and of Judaism.

Zionism: A movement to rebuild the Jewish state in Israel; from the word Zion, another name for Jerusalem.

Zoroastrianism: The ancient religion of Persia, developed by the prophet Zoroaster (c. 628–551 B.C.). Believers perform good deeds to help the highest deity, Ahura Mazda, battle the evil spirit Ahriman.

Junior
Worldmark
Encyclopedia of
World Holidays

Easter

Also Known As:
Semana Santa (Colombia, Spain)
Pascha (Greece)
Wielkanoc (Poland)
Velykden (Ukraine)

Introduction

For Christians, Jesus Christ (c. 6 B.C.–c. A.D. 30) is not just the founder of Christianity. According to the Bible, the sacred book of Christianity, he is also the Son of God who came into the world to die for the sins of mankind in order to make peace between God and humanity. The Bible (John 3:16–17) teaches that because Christ died for man's sins and rose from the grave, believers in Christ can also experience eternal life:

> For God so loved the world, that he gave his only begotten Son, that whosoever believeth in him should not perish, but have everlasting life. For God sent not his Son into the world to condemn the world; but that the world through him might be saved.

During Holy Week and Easter, which is considered the most sacred holiday of the Christian year, Christ's resurrection from the dead, and the events leading up to it, are remembered. Holy Week is the last week of Lent, a forty-day period of reflection and preparation for Easter, and immediately precedes Easter Sunday.

Because it occurs near the beginning of spring, Easter and springtime are closely associated. Many plants and flowers return to life at this time of year, and this "rebirth" has come to symbolize for some Christians the new life they have gained through Christ. Churches are usually lavishly decorated, often with Easter lilies and other flowers in the white, green, yellow, and pastel colors of spring. Church bells ring and special church services feature candlelight and music.

Families and communities also celebrate with holiday feasts and Easter egg hunts—the egg is a symbol of new life. A special attraction for young people is a visit by the Easter bunny, who leaves baskets of treats and hides Easter eggs.

History

Easter is the oldest of all the Christian holidays, having become well established by the second century. The origin of its name is not certain, but some believe it came from the Middle English word *ostern*, meaning the direction from which the sun rises; others say it comes from *eostur*, the Norse word for spring, or from *Eostre*, an Anglo-Saxon goddess of spring.

Holiday Fact Box: Easter

Themes

At Easter, Christians around the world rejoice over Jesus Christ's resurrection from the dead two days after he was crucified. During Holy Week, the week before Easter, Christians remember various events leading up to Christ's resurrection: the Thursday before Easter, Maundy Thursday, commemorates the Last Supper of Jesus with his disciples; on Good Friday, the Crucifixion is mourned; and on Sunday, the Resurrection is celebrated.

Type of Holiday

Easter is primarily a religious holiday, the most important and sacred observance in the Christian calendar. Because it occurs in the spring, Easter is also a time to celebrate the return of the warmth of the sun and the reawakening of plant and animal life.

When Celebrated

Easter is a movable feast, celebrated in Western churches on the Sunday following the first full moon after the spring equinox, between March 22 and April 25. If the full moon is on a Sunday, Easter is held the next Sunday. Orthodox churches in the East also stipulate that Easter must be celebrated after Passover, which is also a movable feast, so they may observe Easter one to five weeks later than Western churches.

Easter and Passover

After Jesus Christ's death in approximately A.D. 30, his followers became known as Christians and their new religion was called Christianity. Like Jesus, these new Christians originally were Jews, and while their religion grew, they adopted many aspects of Hebrew religious customs and adapted others.

Easter, in fact, was first commemorated along with the Jewish Passover festival, an observance of the Jews' delivery from slavery in Egypt, as told in the Bible in Chapter 12 of Exodus. The root word *pasch,* from which many words associated with Easter are derived, comes from the Hebrew *pesach,* meaning "passover." Many European Christians call Easter *Pascha.*

At the Passover meal, the early Jews ate a sacrificial lamb, which commemorated an event that happened during their delivery from slavery. According to the Bible, each Jewish family was commanded to smear blood from a sacrificial lamb on their doorway. This sign would cause the angel of death to "pass over" their home. The angel was sent by God to slay the first-born children of the Egyptians, who had kept the Jews in slavery.

Easter is therefore considered by many to be the Christian equivalent of Passover because both commemorate delivery from oppression. Christians believe that just as God freed the Jews from slavery in Egypt, Christ died for their sins and was resurrected, and so freed them from enslavement to sin. There is also a direct calendar connection between the two holidays: according to most authorities, Christ was crucified on Passover Day.

A woman dressed as the Easter bunny participates in an Easter parade in Philadelphia, Pennsylvania, in 1999. Young children in the United States and some European countries eagerly await the Easter bunny, who brings them colored eggs and candy. Reproduced by permission of AP/Wide World Photos.

Easter Day controversy

A controversy arose in the early days of Christianity over the proper date for observing Easter. The question revolved around whether Easter should be celebrated at the same time as Passover on the Jewish calendar, which meant it could fall on any day of the week, or if it should be celebrated only on a Sunday. Christians believed Christ rose from the grave on the Sunday following his death, and so began observing Sunday as their holy day of the week. The Jewish day of rest and worship, called the Sabbath, is Saturday.

In 325, a church governing body known as the Council of Nicaea (pronounced nye-SEE-uh; a city in what is now Turkey) decided on a compromise and decreed that Easter should be celebrated on the Sunday following the first full moon after the spring equinox, March 21. Therefore, Easter in the West falls between March 22 and April 25. An equinox occurs when the length of the day's sunlight is equal to the length of the day's darkness. This happens only twice a year— once in the spring and once in the fall.

The Eastern Orthodox Church says that Easter must also fall after Passover, so

Young girls read from books they created telling the story of Passover at their New York school in 1999. Easter was first commemorated along with the Jewish Passover festival, an observance of the Jews' delivery from slavery in Egypt. Reproduced by permission of AP/Wide World Photos.

for this branch of Christianity, Easter is celebrated any time between April 4 and May 8. The Eastern Orthodox Church is a Christian community that split with the Roman Catholic Church. The split started with countries in eastern Europe and western Asia. Today, there are Eastern Orthodox communities in countries all over the world, including the United States.

Weeklong observances

During early celebrations, the Saturday night and Sunday observance of Easter commemorated the events leading up to Christ's death, his crucifixion, and his resurrection as one event. By the end of the fourth century, however, the number of

days devoted to Easter observances had increased to eight.

Palm Sunday: Many churches in Palestine began observing the Sunday before Easter in commemoration of Christ's triumphal entry into the capital city of Jerusalem. According to the Bible, as Christ entered the city, people cheered him, waved palm branches, and lined his path with the branches. Palm branches were considered signs of victory and peace in the New Testament (the second half of the Bible, consisting of Christian writings). The crowds paid him tribute because they believed Jesus Christ was the Messiah, who, according to the Old Testament (the first half of the Bible and the sacred book of Judaism, containing the Hebrew Scriptures), would save the world from sin.

By the ninth century, Palm Sunday celebrations, which were observed by waving and displaying palm branches, were also common in Europe. In countries without palms, branches from other trees were used. Waving palm branches and singing songs of celebration on Palm Sunday were part of a growing Easter tradition of imitating as closely as possible the last days of Christ's life.

On the Monday following Palm Sunday, Christians began commemorating the biblical story of the cleansing of the temple, when Jesus drove out the moneychangers. Tuesday became the day to remember the incident related in Matthew 22:15–21 when the church leaders tried to trick Christ. And Wednesday came to be known as "Spy Wednesday," the day that Judas, one of Jesus' closest followers, agreed to betray Jesus for thirty pieces of silver.

Maundy Thursday: By the end of the fourth century, Christians began to observe the Thursday before Easter in memory of the Last Supper. This final supper of Christ with his followers was probably a Passover meal (Mark 14:16). During this meal, Jesus started the custom of Holy Communion (Mark 14:22–25). Holy Communion is a Christian ritual that involves eating bread and wine that has been blessed in memory of Christ's death:

> And as they did eat, Jesus took bread, and blessed, and brake it, and gave to them, and said, Take, eat: this is my body. And he took the cup, and when he had given thanks, he gave it to them: and they all drank of it. And he said unto them, This is my blood of the new testament, which is shed for many.

During the Middle Ages (c. 500–1500), this Thursday became known as Maundy Thursday, a term that may come from *mandatum novum* (new commandment), referring to Jesus' commandment to his disciples on that day to "love one another" (John 13:34–35):

> A new commandment I give unto you, That ye love one another; as I have loved you, that ye also love one another. By this shall all men know that ye are my disciples, if ye have love one to another.

Good Friday: The Friday following Maundy Thursday was the day that Christ was killed, and was called Good Friday. The origin of the name "Good Friday" is also unclear, but one notion is that "Good Friday" may have once been "God's" Friday. Another theory is that "good" refers to the good gift that Christ gave to all people when he died on the cross.

Good Friday, also known as Holy Friday or Great Friday in some countries, became the day for venerating (showing respect for) the cross. This practice evolved into a ceremony known as "Creeping to the Cross." A replica of the cross was displayed while people sang: "Behold the wood of the cross, on which hung the salvation of the world; come let us adore."

Holy Saturday and Easter Sunday: By the end of the fourth century, Holy Saturday, like the Holy Week days before it, became a separate day of remembrance. It marked the day after Christ's death and the day before his resurrection, when he lay in his tomb. Known as the Easter Vigil, the celebration occurred on the night of Holy Saturday (Easter Eve) and lasted until early Easter Sunday.

From at least the third century, Holy Saturday was a popular time for baptisms, because baptism symbolizes the "washing away" of sins and the "resurrection" of a sinner into a new life in Christ. People who were newly baptized wore white clothes, so white became the color most associated with Easter. Holy Saturday also became the day for new converts to receive their first Holy Communion.

Paschal Sunday (Easter Day), the most important and joyful day in the Christian calendar, became a celebration of Christ's resurrection. One of the first occurrences of an Easter Day parade was noted as early as the beginning of the fourth century when Roman Emperor Constantine the Great (ruled 306–37) ordered the members of his court to wear their best clothes to celebrate Easter Sunday. Constantine had converted to Christianity and figured prominently in the spread of the religion because he gave his fellow Christians protection from persecution.

"The Night of Illumination"

From the time of the first Easter celebration, Easter Eve Saturday was a night of prayer known as the Easter Vigil. Light played a very important role in this observance. In addition to illuminating churches with hundreds of candles, people used dozens of lights in their homes. They carried candles in the streets, and even lit up entire towns and villages with torches and lamps. Hilltops blazed with fires that could be seen for miles.

Large candles and candlelight processions, representing Christ as "the Light of the World," also became popular. In ancient times, great Paschal candles weighing up to three hundred pounds were used in Spain, Gaul (present-day France), Italy, and probably Africa. Church members used the Paschal candle to light their own candles, which they then carried home to use in special ceremonies. Poems about these candles and about "Christ the light" were also composed. The most famous, the *Exultet,* was written in the seventh century or earlier.

Because of these lights, Easter Eve became known as "The Night of Illumination." After the gloom and despair of Good Friday, when churches and houses were darkened, Christians were ready for the brightness of Easter Eve. The illumination represented the victory of light over darkness, of salvation over sin, of eternal life over death.

Easter today

Most of the religious symbolism and many of the traditional customs associated with Easter were established by the end of the Middle Ages (c. 1500). These symbols and observances are still acknowledged and practiced today, with variations among the different branches of Christianity.

Folklore, Legends, Stories

The story of Jesus Christ's death and resurrection as told in the Bible provides the central theme for the celebration of Easter. The story is told in all four of the Gospels, the first four books of the New Testament: Matthew, Mark, Luke, and John. Other Easter legends that developed over the centuries usually have some connection with the events that occurred during the last week of Jesus' life.

The Easter story

Jesus Christ grew up in the town of Nazareth near the Sea of Galilee. As a young man, he was a carpenter. When he was about thirty years old, he began teaching and performing miracles, such as healing the sick. He soon attracted twelve disciples, or followers, who traveled with him on his journeys. Many of those who heard him and witnessed his miracles believed he was the Messiah, or Savior, promised in the Bible.

On the Sunday before he was crucified, Jesus rode into the capital city of Jerusalem accompanied by his disciples. Because his reputation for teaching and performing miracles had become so great, he was greeted by a great crowd who waved and spread palm branches and garments in his path.

Over the next few days, the religious leaders and the Romans who ruled the area became alarmed as Christ's influence and followers rapidly increased. Afraid that Jesus was becoming too powerful, the priests began accusing him of breaking religious laws. Finally, they agreed to give Judas Iscariot, one of Christ's twelve disciples, thirty pieces of silver to betray him and reveal his whereabouts to the Romans.

On Thursday, Christ and his disciples celebrated the Last Supper, which was believed to be a Passover meal. Then Jesus went to the Garden of Gethsemane to pray. While Jesus was praying, Judas led Roman soldiers to the garden to arrest him. Judas identified Jesus to the soldiers with a kiss.

Jesus was convicted of blasphemy (denying things the priests held sacred), nailed to a cross to die, and buried on Friday. During this time, crucifixion, or being nailed to a cross, was a common Roman method of execution. On Saturday, his body rested in a tomb donated by a follower. Because Jesus had said that he would rise from the tomb on the third day after his

An archbishop of the Armenian Church in America releases a dove during Easter celebrations on the steps of New York's Saint Vartan Cathedral in 1999. Twelve doves were set free, symbolizing Jesus Christ's sending out twelve apostles to preach to the world. Reproduced by permission of AP/Wide World Photos.

death, the priests convinced the Roman governor to seal the tomb with a huge stone and post guards to prevent Jesus' followers from stealing the body and claiming he had risen from the dead.

On Easter Sunday, some of Jesus' followers went to visit his tomb. According to the Gospel of Matthew:

> Suddenly there was a great earthquake; for an angel of the Lord, descending from heaven, came and rolled back

the stone and sat on it. His appearance was like lightning, and his clothing white as snow. For fear of him the guards shook and became like dead men. But the angel said to the women, 'Do not be afraid; I know that you are looking for Jesus who was crucified. He is not here; for he has been raised, as he said.'

Flying church bells

One of the oldest stories told to European Catholic children about Easter concerns church bells. According to legend, church bells fly away to Rome to be blessed by the pope, the head of the Roman Catholic Church, on Maundy Thursday. They fly back again on Holy Saturday. During their flight, the church bells drop colored Easter eggs for all good children.

Another Easter tradition is that church bells were stopped from ringing on Maundy Thursday and Good Friday because Christians were mourning the Crucifixion. In many parts of Europe, church bells are replaced with wooden rattles and clappers until they are allowed to begin ringing again at midnight on Holy Saturday or on Easter Day.

Easter legends

A popular Easter legend is that of the dogwood tree, the wood of which Jesus' cross was said to be made. The dogwood was once a tall, strong tree with hard wood. But after the tree realized that its wood was used in the Crucifixion, it mourned. Christ took pity on it and made it grow small and slender, with curving limbs. He caused its flowers to grow in the shape of a cross, with brownish nail prints at the four ends and a center shaped like Christ's crown of thorns. From that day, the dogwood would be remembered as a sacred tree, a symbol of Easter and Christianity.

Another legend says that the robin red breast got its color after it flew down to pluck a thorn from Christ's brow as he carried the cross. A drop of Jesus' blood fell on the robin's breast, coloring it red for all time.

Customs, Traditions, Ceremonies

Holy Week is a time for observing the oldest of Christian customs. Many of the rituals of the Catholic and Eastern Orthodox churches date from as early as the first and second centuries. The term Holy Week was first used by Catholic churches in the West during the fourth century. It was called Great Week in Eastern churches of the same period.

Palm Sunday

The Sunday before Easter Sunday is commemorated as the day Jesus rode triumphantly into Jerusalem on a donkey. His followers lined his path with palm branches, the Roman custom of welcoming victorious armies home from battle. Others waved palm fronds as he passed by to welcome him to the city.

To remember this day, Christians carry palm branches or the branches of another representative plant, such as the pussy willow, to church on Palm Sunday to be blessed. Sometimes, palm fronds are woven into crosses and other shapes and hung in Christian homes. These shaped palm fronds are believed to protect the household from fire and storm.

In Greece, priests give each member of the congregation a *vaya,* a small cross woven from a palm branch with a sprig of bay or myrtle attached. In Rome, the pope blesses the palms in the world's largest

Palm Sunday procession. Afterward, these palms are burned. The ashes are saved to mark the foreheads of the congregation on the following year's Ash Wednesday, the day that marks the beginning of Lent.

Holy Monday and Tuesday

In Latin American countries and in Spain, Holy Week processions begin as early as Holy Monday and increase in size each day. On the morning of Holy Tuesday, people in some parts of Colombia take a feast to prisoners. On Holy Thursday, one prisoner is chosen for release and is given his freedom. This is done to commemorate the biblical story of Barabbas, a prisoner in ancient Jerusalem who was guilty of murder. It was tradition during the Passover ceremonies that the citizens could choose one prisoner to be set free; the crowd chose Barabbas instead of Jesus.

Maundy Thursday

In many churches, Maundy, or Holy, Thursday is a day for taking Holy Communion in memory of the Last Supper. After Holy Thursday church services, the period of mourning Jesus' death begins. In many countries, church bells stop ringing and are not heard again until midnight on Holy Saturday or on Easter Sunday. Altar candles are put out, and altars are cleaned and left bare until Saturday.

Holy Thursday is an important day for candlelight processions in many Spanish Catholic countries. In Ukraine, women stay up late on the night of Holy Thursday, quietly making *pysanky,* Easter eggs.

Good Friday

Good Friday is remembered as the day Jesus was crucified. On this day in the

Poems and Stories About Easter

"The Loveliest Rose in the World" (story, 1852) by Hans Christian Andersen

"Ballad of Trees and the Master" (poem, 1880) by Sidney Lanier

"The Selfish Giant" (story, 1888) by Oscar Wilde

"The White Blackbird" (story, 1924) by Padraic Colum

"Easter Morning" (poem, 1946) by Aileen Fisher

"Candles at Midnight" (story, 1947) by Alice Geer Kelsey

Catholic Church, altars and religious statues are covered with mourning cloths, and no mass is said. People attend a solemn ceremony called the Veneration of the Cross. In Orthodox churches in Ukraine, worshipers kiss the Holy Shroud, a specially woven and embroidered cloth that represents Jesus' burial cloth. In Greek Orthodox churches, parishioners decorate a kind of coffin with flowers and carry it in a procession through the streets.

Good Friday processions represent the funeral of Christ. In Latin America and Spain, these processions are quiet and somber. Many are held at night, by candlelight, and the smell of burning incense fills the air. Strong men carry life-size carved wooden figures of Christ, the Virgin Mary (the mother of Jesus), and other scenes from the Passion (suffering) of Christ.

Many of these figures are centuries-old works of religious art. They are beautifully painted, dressed in fine garments, and ornamented with jewels.

In Poland, churches build a mock tomb for Good Friday. People stay by the tombs, keeping a symbolic watch for Jesus' resurrection. On Good Friday, church services are held from noon until three in the afternoon, the hours during which Christ is said to have suffered on the cross before his death. This service is called the *Tre Ore* (Three Hours).

Many Christians build bonfires on Good Friday and burn straw effigies, or representative figures, of Judas Iscariot. In Mexico, children sometimes hit a "Judas" piñata, which then spills out candy. In Greece and some other countries, people break pottery on Good Friday, saying each shard "cuts" Judas.

Holy Saturday

Holy Saturday is said to be the day when Christ rested in the tomb. For many Christians, this is a quiet day for fasting and preparing colored eggs and special foods for the Easter Sunday feast. In Ukraine and Poland, Holy Saturday is the day for blessing baskets of food to be consumed on Easter Sunday.

Saturday night, however, holds the biggest celebration in Eastern Orthodox churches. Many Catholic churches conduct a midnight mass on Holy Saturday, once known as the Night of Illumination. Candles, representing Christ as "the Light of the World," are widely used in all of these services. In Catholic churches, the huge Paschal (Easter) candle is lit, along with five pieces of incense representing the five wounds that Christ received before his death. This candle-lighting ceremony dates to at least the fourth century.

After Christ's resurrection is proclaimed at midnight, members of Orthodox congregations turn to one another with the traditional greeting, "Christ is risen!" The response is, "He is risen indeed!"

Easter Sunday

Easter Sunday, the day Christ rose from the dead, is a day of rejoicing for all Christians. Because it is believed that Christ rose from the grave at dawn, many Protestant churches hold sunrise services on Easter Sunday morning. According to legend, one can see the shape of the Lamb of God in the sun at dawn on Easter Sunday.

In Greece and many Latin American countries, Easter Sunday is a big feast day, with folk dancing and fiestas. Polish families celebrate Easter Sunday with a bounteous Easter breakfast feast after the long fast of Lent.

Reenacting the Passion of Christ

Christians began reenacting the last days of Christ, called "the Passion," as early as the first and second centuries in Jerusalem, where the events took place. Modern "Passion plays" had their beginning in church masses of about the tenth century, when priests re-created these events. They became increasingly popular in Germany, Italy, France, Spain, Holland, and England. Chants and music were added as they evolved into the magnificent plays presented today.

The world's most famous Passion play is presented every tenth year in Oberammergau (pronounced oh-buhr-AHlt-muh-gow), a village in Germany's Bavarian Alps,

These Finnish girls dressed as witches are following a Palm Sunday tradition of going door to door offering pussy willow branches as a token of goodwill in exchange for payment.
Reproduced by permission of AP/Wide World Photos.

where it has been a tradition since 1634. The people of the village promised to create the play to show their gratitude to God for allowing them to survive a plague that killed thousands in Germany during that time.

Clothing, Costumes

The custom of wearing new spring clothing on Easter Sunday probably dates back as early as the fourth century. At that time, those who were baptized during the Easter Vigil, which began on the evening of Holy Saturday and continued into Easter Sunday, wore white robes as symbols of their new life in Christ. Those who had already been baptized wore new clothes on Easter Sunday to show they had a new life as well.

Easter parades became common during the Middle Ages in Europe, when people walked up and down the streets in new clothes after mass on Easter Sunday. They sometimes formed an Easter procession, led by someone carrying a crucifix.

In the United States, during the late nineteenth and early twentieth centuries, New York City became famous for its Easter parade on Fifth Avenue. The Easter bonnet became popular during the early twentieth century, when women wore new spring-time hats to church on Easter Sunday.

People in many parts of the world wear folk costumes on Easter Sunday to perform traditional dances for the festive occasion. In Holy Week processions, elaborate costumes are placed on the life-size figures carried on top of decorated platforms. These figures represent Jesus, his mother Mary, and other characters from the Passion of Christ. The individuals who carry the statues wear hooded robes. Other traditional garments worn on Easter Sunday include the bright gold robes of the priests who perform the Resurrection service in Orthodox churches.

Foods, Recipes

Foods prepared for the Easter Sunday feast include many of those that are forbidden during Lent, the forty-day preparation for Easter that involves fasting and doing without certain foods, such as eggs, many meats, butter, and cheese. For most, eggs are probably the first food that comes to mind when thinking of Easter.

In Ukraine, the head of the household cuts a boiled egg into pieces, one for each family member, at the start of the Easter Sunday feast. This egg is one of the foods that was blessed by a priest in church the night before. Some eastern European Christians once believed that God would punish them if they ate Easter foods before they were blessed.

Roast lamb has been a traditional Easter food since the ninth century, when it became the pope's main Easter dish. Lamb is also particularly associated with Easter because Jesus is called the sacrificial lamb of God, or the Paschal lamb. In Poland, people make a small lamb from sugar and butter or bread dough as a centerpiece for the Easter table. In Greece, lamb is roasted outdoors on a spit for a traditional Greek Easter Sunday feast.

Easter breads, such as the Ukrainian *paska* (pronounced POS-kuh); the Polish Easter cake, *babka* (pronounced BOB-kuh); and the Greek *lambropsoma* (pronounced lahm-brop-SOH-muh); are traditional foods. Hot cross buns, made with raisins and frosted with a cross shape, have been a traditional Good Friday food in Great Britain and other countries for hundreds of years.

Arts, Crafts, Games

Much of the world's great religious art is based on the Passion and Resurrection of Jesus Christ. Beginning in the fifth century, the cross was used in Christian art. Painters began depicting scenes from the Crucifixion around the seventh century. The Western world's most well-known religious painting is the *Last Supper,* a large mural painted on the wall of a small church in Italy by Leonardo da Vinci (1452–1519).

In Greece and Poland, people visit and pray before religious icons, religious images or scenes painted on wood. A monastery in Poland houses the famous icon known as "the Black Madonna," which is said to have been painted by the biblical Saint Luke as he talked with Christ's mother, Mary. Many people believe that God works miracles through these sacred representations. In Latin American countries and Spain, the lifelike wooden figures represented in Holy Week processions are among the most valuable works of art and are greatly treasured.

Egg art

Coloring and decorating Easter eggs is a folk art that has developed over the centuries. Greeks color eggs red in honor of the blood of Christ. Ukrainians and people from Poland decorate eggs using a batik (pronounced ba-TEEK) method in which intricate designs are drawn and the egg is dyed one color at a time. These world-famous Easter eggs are called *pysanky*. Another Polish method is to cut designs from paper, which are then fastened to the egg with glue. Today, eggs are dyed with commercial food colors, but in earlier times people used natural materials such as onion skins, beets, and flowers to make dyes.

Easter eggs can also be made from a variety of materials, including marble, wood, and glass. Some glass eggs have hollow centers in which miniature nature scenes can be viewed. European rulers once had elaborate artificial eggs designed, many gold-plated and bejeweled, to give as gifts to their loyal officers. These eggs were often filled with small presents. During the late 1800s, Russian jeweler Peter Carl Fabergé (1846–1920) designed jeweled Easter eggs for Russian royalty. These eggs are considered valuable works of art.

Egg games

Many Easter games are played with Easter eggs. Some of these are egg rolling, egg hunts, and egg fights. In an egg roll, children see who can roll an egg the farthest down a grassy hill, or who can roll an egg without breaking it. In some countries, when children roll eggs down the hill they try to hit other eggs as they reach the bottom. Egg rolling is sometimes said to recall the stone being rolled away from Christ's tomb.

In an egg hunt, adults hide the Easter eggs, telling small children they were hidden by the Easter bunny. The eggs may be hidden in the house or outdoors. The child who finds the most eggs gets a prize, usually candy.

In an egg fight, two people each hold an Easter egg vertically, one on top of the other. The person whose egg is on top uses the bottom end of his egg to tap the top end of his opponent's bottom egg. The competition continues until one person comes away with an uncracked egg. In one traditional Greek Easter game, an egg hangs from the ceiling on a string. A player bops the egg with his head to start it swinging; he then tries to catch the egg in his mouth.

Symbols

Most Easter symbols, like the majority of Easter traditions and customs, originated with the biblical story of Christ's death and resurrection. The symbols that are most associated with Easter include crosses, which recall the cross that Jesus Christ was nailed to; the lamb, which represents Jesus, the Lamb of God; Easter eggs, symbols of new life; the Easter rabbit, also symbolic of new life and rebirth; and Easter lilies.

The cross

The cross on which Christ was crucified has become the foremost symbol of Easter. The cross was declared the symbol of Christianity by the Council of Nicaea in 325, which also set the date for Easter observances.

Three crosses are often displayed in churches at Easter and throughout the year. The center cross is the largest of the three and belongs to Christ; the two smaller crosses were used for two thieves who were crucified along with him. In Jesus' day, crucifixion was a method used by the Romans to execute slaves and certain criminals. But with Jesus' death, the cross became a symbol of hope and, for Christians, represents God's love for mankind and the promise of eternal life.

In an early Christian Good Friday ceremony, the actual cross on which Jesus was crucified was placed in an ornamental casket. Church members approached the cross one by one, touched it with their foreheads, and then kissed it. This was the beginning of the Catholic Church ritual of Good Friday known as the Veneration of the Cross.

In Holy Week processions in Spain, the Philippines, and Central and South America, people called "penitents" carry heavy wooden crosses on their backs. They sometimes have themselves actually nailed briefly to a cross—in a gesture of repentance for their sins and in thanksgiving for Christ's gift to humanity.

The lamb

The lamb was an important sacrificial animal throughout biblical Old Testament times. Often depicted on a banner with a cross, the *Angus Dei* (Lamb of God) represents Jesus and associates his death with that of the lambs at the first Passover. The crucified Jesus was later referred to as the Paschal (Passover) lamb, whose blood was shed for the sins of mankind. Jesus Christ is referred to in the Bible as "the Lamb of God who takes away the sins of the world" (John 1:29).

Easter eggs

Long before Christianity, ancient peoples considered the egg a source of life and a symbol of spring. The Easter egg, however, has been given a Christian meaning. Red-colored eggs, such as those colored in Greece, are said to represent Christ's blood. The eggshell represents Christ's tomb, and when the egg is cracked, it represents Christ's resurrection. Cracking an Easter egg is also said to represent Christians' breaking the bonds of sin and death through their belief in Christ.

Coloring and decorating eggs is a major part of secular (nonreligious) Easter celebrations, as are games played with eggs. In Ukraine, Poland, and other Eastern European countries, women and girls have developed egg decorating into an art, with the beautiful and colorful pysanky. Colored and decorated eggs are taken to church to be blessed on Holy Saturday in both the Eastern Orthodox and the Catholic Churches of Europe.

In Italy and other parts of southern Europe, dozens of colored eggs are placed in a bowl and given as gifts to those who come visiting on Easter Sunday. In Germany, colored eggs are sometimes fastened to the bare branches of a tree to make an Easter egg tree. People in German communities in the United States have kept this custom as well.

Easter rabbit or hare

The hare was a pre-Christian symbol of fertility in many cultures. Folklore about the Easter hare became popular in Germany during the late 1500s, when the

Children hunt for eggs the day before Easter 1995 in New Berlin, Illinois. In an egg hunt, the child who finds the most eggs gets a prize, usually candy. Reproduced by permission of AP/Wide World Photos.

animal was said to lay red eggs on Holy Thursday and multicolored eggs on Holy Saturday night. Some say the notion of a hare or rabbit laying eggs might have come from a bird called the plover, which had a habit of laying its eggs in rabbits' nests. During the 1800s, German bakers were the first to make Easter rabbit pastries.

Germans called the Easter hare "Oschter Haws," who was said to lay a nest full of colored eggs for children who were well behaved. Children built nests for the Easter bunny in barns or near their homes and found them filled with colored eggs on Easter Sunday morning. These nests later became Easter baskets, which parents filled with colored eggs and candies while young children were sleeping. The nest-building custom was also popular in Ukraine and other eastern European countries. In some countries, children put out their hats or bonnets for the Easter bunny to use as nests.

Easter lily

The lily is a prominent figure in the Easter story. The oldest-known lily was a plant with bell-shaped or funnel-shaped white flowers that grew in northern Palestine, the area where Jesus lived. It was called the Madonna lily because paintings often show Jesus' mother Mary holding the delicate flowers.

The first type of lily to be associated with Christ's Passion and Crucifixion was the lily of the field, or windflower, which was also native to the region where Jesus lived. This lily blooms in red, white, pink, and purple. According to legend, the red blooms grew at the foot of the cross and were stained with the blood of Christ. Another lily, called the lily of the valley, does not grow near Jerusalem, but legend says this white flower grew wherever Mary's tears fell to the ground as she wept for her son, Jesus.

The white trumpet lily, called the Easter lily, is known as a symbol of purity and of the Resurrection. It was introduced to the United States during the late 1800s from Bermuda. Because it blooms during the Easter season, the trumpet lily has been cultivated and sold for many years to decorate churches and homes at Easter time.

Music, Dance

Devotional music is most associated with Easter. In Colombia and many other Latin American countries, musicians playing hymns walk in Holy Week processions. During Good Friday processions in Spain, a spectator may suddenly sing a *saeta* (arrow), a brief, loud song of mourning that "pierces" the heart of those who hear it.

Latin hymns are traditional at Easter mass in Catholic and Orthodox churches. Nineteenth-century translator John Mason Neale (1818–1866) made old Greek and Latin Easter hymns available to modern-day people through his translations. He published *Carols for Eastertide* in 1854 and

wrote the much-loved Easter hymn "The World Itself":

The world itself keeps Easter Day,
And Easter larks are singing;
And Easter flowers are blooming gay,
And Easter buds are springing.
Alleluia, alleluia.
The Lord of all things lives anew,
And all His works are living too.
Alleluia, alleluia.

Oratorios (long choral pieces without action or scenery) were developed in Italy in the mid-sixteenth century, when hymns were sung to accompany the reenactment of scenes from the Bible. German-born composer George Frideric Handel (1685–1759) wrote the oratorio *Messiah,* with its famous *Hallelujah Chorus.* Handel also wrote the Easter hymn "I Know That My Redeemer Liveth." Passion music developed in Germany, where it was sung only in churches to accompany Passion plays about the Resurrection and Crucifixion.

"The Palms," by French opera singer and composer Jean-Baptiste Faure (1830–1914), is a popular hymn sung in Protestant churches on Palm Sunday. *The Saint Matthew Passion,* by German composer Johann Sebastian Bach (1685–1750), is sung by choirs at Catholic masses on Palm Sunday.

On Good Friday, Catholics sing Bach's *St. John Passion,* considered one of the greatest Easter compositions. *The Seven Last Words,* by Austrian composer Joseph Haydn (1732–1809), is also sung on Good Friday. In Protestant churches, a favorite hymn sung on Easter Sunday is "Christ the Lord Is Ris'n Today," written by English religious leader Charles Wesley (1707–1788).

Popular Easter songs include "Easter Parade," written in 1933 by American composer Irving Berlin, and the "Bunny Hop," a children's dance song.

Special Role of Children, Young Adults

Children and young adults play important roles in Holy Week processions in Spain, Greece, and Latin American countries. They may walk in processions with adults, perhaps carrying candles or incense, or they may carry palms in Palm Sunday processions. Youth who attend Orthodox churches carry special candles to Easter Vigil services held on Holy Saturday night. In Popayán, Colombia, children have their own processions, in which they carry small replicas of the holy statues carried by adults.

Greek children help decorate the Epitaphion (pronounced eh-puh-TAFF-ee-uhn), a representation of Christ's tomb, with flowers for their town's Good Friday procession. Greek girls dress in folk costumes and do folk dances for Easter Sunday celebrations. In towns where a "burning of Judas" rite is held, children may help build the Judas figure and gather wood for the bonfire.

Christian young people in most countries attend church services with their parents throughout Holy Week and on Easter Sunday. Many also participate in Lenten fasting during the weeks leading up to Easter. Since many schools break for a holiday at Easter, children and their families often visit grandparents and other relatives. This period has also become a time for families to take vacations, especially to beaches.

Young children in the United States and some European countries wait eagerly for the Easter bunny's arrival on Easter Sunday morning. They believe the legendary rabbit will bring colored eggs and candy to fill their Easter baskets. Youngsters help dye Easter eggs during the days before Easter. They go on egg hunts, have egg fights, and play egg games on Easter Sunday.

Colombia

Name of Holiday: Semana Santa

Introduction

The Catholic Church plays a major role in Colombia, which has been called one of the most Catholic countries in the Western Hemisphere. Colombians observe Easter and Holy Week according to strict rituals, many dating to the 1500s and 1600s. Holy Week, called Semana Santa (pronounced say-MAH-nuh SAHN-tuh), is Colombia's most important holiday. People attend long church services and participate in numerous parades or processions commemorating the Passion, the Crucifixion, and the Resurrection of Jesus Christ.

History

Colombians are a people of Indian, Spanish, and African origin. Most are Roman Catholics, a religion the Spanish explorers and their accompanying priests introduced to Colombia during the early sixteenth century. The Spanish priests converted the native Indians of Latin America to Christianity and later also converted the African slaves brought to work the mines and plantations.

The priests emphasized church ritual, because it was a way for the native Indians and Africans to see the new religion in practice. The new Christian rituals replaced or sometimes co-existed with native rituals and ceremonies. Among these new Christian practices were the Holy Week processions and masses that have been held in parts of Colombia since the mid-1500s.

A town founded and rebuilt on tradition

Popayán (pronounced poh-puh-YAHN), a city with magnificent colonial architecture, is the premier site for Holy Week processions in Colombia. Holy Week ceremonies began in Popayán around 1558. During the centuries that followed, if Colombia was at war, peace was declared for Holy Week so that processions could still be held.

On Holy Thursday in 1983, Popayán was struck by the worst earthquake in its history. Its most beautiful churches and a revered statue of Christ crumbled to the ground. Some three hundred people were killed, many as they worshiped in the cathedrals. That night, the bell that always rang to announce the arrival of Holy Week tolled for the loss experienced by so many people. Without electricity, candlelight filled the valley and town. There was no Holy Thursday procession that night, but the people of Popayán vowed to make the next year's Holy Week the most beautiful ever.

Instead of building new, modern buildings, the citizens used money for reconstruction to rebuild historical churches, museums, monuments, and universities. They wanted the streets to look the same as they always did during the Holy Week processions and during other traditional events held throughout the year. Today, it

is said that one can hardly tell an earthquake once shattered the beautiful town. And thousands of pilgrims and tourists from all over Colombia and from around the world converge on the city each year to celebrate Holy Week.

Other Colombian cities with a long history of noted Easter celebrations include Barranquilla (pronounced bar-uhn-KEE-yuh) and Zipaquirá (pronounced zee-puh-kih-RAH).

Folklore, Legends, Stories

Because Holy Week activities have been celebrated in Colombia since the 1500s, many of the legends surrounding them date to at least the sixteenth century. The following legends are based on the history of Popayán. One is about a famous statesman and the other is about Colombian Indians who were surprised and frightened by an early Holy Week procession.

The outlaw *carguero*

One Colombian legend tells about General José María Obando (1795–1861), a Popayán statesman and gentleman who had become an enemy of the state and was sought by officials. Obando had the honor of being a *carguero* (kar-GAY-roh), a bearer of one of the statues carried in Holy Week processions. This honor had been passed down from father to son in his family. In spite of the danger of being caught, Obando took his place as a bearer of the statue *Our Lady of Sorrows* in the Good Friday procession. The people and the officials admired him so much for his devotion that they let him participate in the procession and afterward get away.

The "fiery creature" that prevented attack

Another legend concerns a band of Colombian Indians who were preparing to attack Popayán during the late sixteenth century. As they watched from a hilltop, they saw a long line of fire moving through the streets of the city. The Indians did not know the line of fire was actually a Holy Week procession, lit by thousands of candles. They believed it was a fiery creature coming to kill them, and so they fled, abandoning their planned attack.

Customs, Traditions, Ceremonies

During the weeks before Easter, Colombian families clean and repaint their homes in pastel pinks, greens, blues, and yellows. Whole communities work together to spruce up churches and churchyards. They wash religious statues and place fresh flowers around them. Priests bring out silver and gold religious objects studded with jewels, many of them dating to the time of Spanish rule. Each church brings out its carved, painted, and decorated life-size wooden statues of scenes from the Passion (sufferings) of Christ. These are made ready for the Holy Week processions, when they are decorated and carried through town.

During Holy Week, Colombian Catholics attend mass each day. In small villages, priests visit homes and bless the household. Easter comes near the end of summer in Colombia, and many families choose this time to take vacations. City dwellers travel to the mountains, the countryside, or the beach, and villagers go to

Underground Holy Week Services

Special Holy Week services are held in the old Colombian city of Zipaquirá (pronounced zee-puh-kih-RAH) in the famous Cathedral of Salt. The original cathedral was carved by miners in 1954 from a centuries-old salt mine that was no longer productive. By 1992, the structure had become unsafe because it flooded during heavy rains. The cathedral was closed until a new one was carved using modern equipment, under the direction of an architect.

The new Cathedral of Salt was opened to visitors in 1995, and can accommodate up to eight hundred worshipers. Mass is held in the new cathedral every Sunday and on holidays. It is also used for special services such as christenings and weddings. The cathedral's ceiling arches to seventy-five feet, and its altar is made from an eighteen-ton block of salt.

the cities to watch the large Holy Week processions.

Week of Dolores procession in Mompós

In the colonial town of Mompós, the week before Holy Week is called the Week of Dolores (pain, grief, or sorrow). Processions that accompany these religious observances have been held in the town since the early 1600s. They begin on Thursday night before Palm Sunday, with the procession of the Despedimiento (dess-pay-duh-me-EN-toe; leave-taking). During the procession, a "stolen" religious image is carried through the streets. The Cross of Mompós, which is kept in one of the town's six historical churches, is also used in the Holy Thursday procession, along with other sacred images.

The proceedings begin at 11 P.M., when the townspeople march to the Church of Saint Francis. They are led by a group of honorable men known as the *nazarenos* (pronounced nah-zuh-RAY-nohs), who will carry the statue in the procession. The people pretend to beat the church door down by kicking it and hitting it with stones and sticks. Once inside, they "steal" one of the holy statues. The nazarenos carry the statue on a wooden platform to the next church in the procession, where a special mass is held.

After the special mass, the procession of the Despedimiento begins, at about 2 A.M. on Friday. Members of the congregation carry candles and slowly march to sacred music, stopping to visit at each of the town's six churches. By 8 A.M., the procession reaches the final church, and another special mass is held.

Palm Sunday mass and processions

In most Colombian cities and towns, people bring palm fronds they have woven into crosses and other designs to masses held on Palm Sunday morning. They also wave palm fronds during the church services, just as people waved palm fronds to welcome Jesus to Jerusalem in the New Testament Bible story. After mass, the priest blesses each palm frond. The people take the branches home and hang them up to protect the household from harm.

Palm Sunday processions begin during the afternoon. In addition to sacred statues, the processions include drum corps and military bands, schoolchildren in uniforms, and rows of people waving palms, white flags, and banners. People shout to proclaim "Jesus the King" and commemorate his entrance into Jerusalem.

Palm Sunday in Popayán

Popayán's Palm Sunday celebrations have been compared with those of Seville, Spain. Thousands of people come from all over Colombia and the world to watch the candlelight processions. Many kneel in the streets to pray as the figures of saints and life-size images of scenes from the Passion of Christ pass by. The platforms on which the holy figures are carried are beautifully decorated.

The men who carry the heavy statues are called cargueros. They are respected citizens who pass the honor of being a bearer down from father to son. The cargueros organize the Palm Sunday procession, which begins at the Chapel of Bethlehem. Only two sacred figures are carried during the procession, a figure of Christ and one of the Virgin Mary, Jesus' mother.

Releasing "Barabbas"

On the morning of Holy Tuesday, an old custom called the Feast of the Prisoners begins. Government officials, priests, the army band, and schoolgirls march to the prison in Popayán. Included in the procession are platforms loaded with prepared food. All the prisoners come into the courtyard for a Holy Week feast

Lent and Holy Week Traditions That Endanger Nature

Although eating meat and eggs is prohibited during Lent in many Catholic churches in South America, eating the meat of reptiles is permitted. In March 1998, the Colombian government launched a campaign warning Colombians that eating the meat and eggs of certain reptiles was putting some animals in danger of extinction.

Many rural Colombians were cutting open the stomachs of live iguanas (a type of large lizard) to take their eggs, often leaving the iguanas to die. People hunting the Icotea tortoise for its meat were burning swamps and wetlands to force the turtles out, destroying the animals and their habitats. The black caiman (an alligator-like reptile) was used as a fish substitute during Lent, and its skin was sold in other countries.

To prevent poachers from further endangering these wild animals, the Colombian government planned to establish "farms" where iguanas, caimans, and Icotea tortoises could be bred and raised for meat and eggs. These products could be then be available for purchase at supermarkets.

The wax palm that grows in the Colombian highlands was also in danger of extinction, because so many were cut to use in Palm Sunday processions. The government suggested people use other, more plentiful, plants such as wheat, corn, or grass, or even white handkerchiefs, in the processions.

and a ceremony based on the biblical story of Barabbas.

In ancient times, it was a custom that during the Passover festival one prisoner could be released from jail: the crowd chose to set free Barabbas, a known murderer, instead of Jesus. In the Holy Tuesday ceremony, one prisoner who has almost completed his sentence is chosen from among all the prisoners. On Holy Thursday, he is stationed on the street, still guarded, and people passing by give him food and money. He is set free that evening.

Candlelight processions

The first evening candlelight procession in Popayán is held on Holy Tuesday. A man with a broom walks ahead of the procession, clearing the streets and "sweeping away evil." After him come acolytes, or attendants, with tinkling bells and vessels filled with burning incense. Then come the cargueros, who bear the holy figures, each man lifting part of his statue's weight with one of the poles attached to a platform.

Many men, women, and children walk alongside the cargueros, carrying candles to illuminate the procession. These marchers are called *alumbrantes* (providers of light). Also in the processions are formally dressed, white-caped members of the religious order Knights of

Burro Beauty Contest

The Colombian town of San Antero holds a contest on Holy Saturday to see which farmer has the most "beautiful" burro. (The burro symbolizes Christ's humble Palm Sunday entrance into Jerusalem on the back of a donkey.) The burros are named after human public figures, such as politicians or entertainers. Farmers dress their female burros in women's dresses and bonnets; male burros wear jackets and trousers. The female burros compete in a swimsuit contest. A king and a queen burro are crowned, and as a prize the winning "couple" is no longer required to work on the farms. The hilarious contest closes with folk dancing, singing, art exhibits, and a fiesta.

the Holy Sepulcher of Jerusalem, an organization of Roman Catholics that originated during the Crusades (religious wars fought primarily during the thirteenth century). Men in tuxedos, wearing white gloves, also walk in the procession carrying wooden crosses. These men are called *regidors*, and it is their job to maintain order and solemnity.

The penitents' procession and Good Friday

On Good Friday, men called "penitents" dress in long brown robes, wear crowns of thorns or leaves, and walk through town in a procession. During the procession, the men perform acts of "penance" both to show sorrow for wrongs they have done during the year and to commemorate Christ's sufferings. Some walk barefoot, or in chains, and carry heavy wooden crosses. Others whip themselves to repent for wrongdoing. Such processions are held in most cities and towns, but Popayán has the most famous and most elaborate ones.

Other processions on Good Friday include holy statues of men removing Christ's body from the cross and of Christ's body being laid in the tomb. As the marchers pass, a small bell is rung slowly, and the cargueros recite the rosary (a Catholic prayer of devotion) in low tones.

Burning Judas and racing to tell Mary

Holy Saturday is the day when many towns and villages burn an effigy, or likeness, of Judas Iscariot, the biblical disciple who betrayed Christ for thirty pieces of silver. The effigy is made from straw, rags, or papier-mâché. It is laced with firecrackers and set on fire in a public place, like the town square. After the fireworks have done their damage, people sometimes beat and drown the bits of leftover "Judas."

In the port city of San Juan, a cargo boat race is held on Holy Saturday. Each boatman pretends to race to see who will be the first to tell Mary that her son Jesus has risen from the dead. When the race is over, a procession begins from the town cathedral.

Throughout Colombia, Holy Saturday is the day for joyful processions of the resurrected Christ. The Easter feast begins on Holy Saturday after nighttime mass.

Easter Sunday is a day for fiestas, feasting, music and dancing, and lighting fireworks.

Clothing, Costumes

Each participant in the Holy Week processions wears a certain garment that identifies his or her role. Cargueros wear long, belted robes, often in white, and pointed hoods. In the town of Mompós, the nazarenos, who carry the holy images in the processions, wear long, blue tunics with hoods that cover the head and face. Holes cut in the hoods allow them to see. A white cord, wrapped several times around the waist, hangs to the ankles. Five tassels representing the wounds of Christ dangle from the ends of the cord. A white cape adorned with a small blue cross covers the nazarenos' shoulders and back.

As in most other countries, people wear their best clothing to Holy Week masses, especially for the Holy Saturday Resurrection services. During Easter Sunday fiestas, people wear folk costumes that can range from Indian or African traditional clothing to early Spanish costumes.

Foods, Recipes

The most popular foods for the Easter feast, held late on Holy Saturday night after mass, are *sopa de maíz* (pronounced SOH-puh day MAH-EES), or corn soup, and *hallacas* (pronounced hah-YAH-kuhs), meat-filled corn tortillas wrapped in plantain (a type of banana) leaves and steamed. Rice or almond pudding is served for dessert. Colombia is famous for its coffee beans, and coffee is the national drink, served at all feasts.

Colombian Corn Soup

Ingredients

3 cups chicken broth

3 cups milk

3 cups corn kernels

1½ cups stewed tomatoes, chopped

2 cloves garlic, chopped

1½ teaspoons ground oregano

salt and pepper to taste

1 to 2 cups shredded cheese (mozzarella, Münster, or Monterey Jack)

Directions

1. Heat all ingredients except cheese together in a large saucepan, stirring until mixture comes to a boil.
2. Reduce heat and simmer for about 10 minutes, stirring often.
3. Remove from heat and stir in cheese until it is melted. Serve soup with warm corn tortillas and hot pepper sauce, if desired.

Arts, Crafts, Games

Life-size wood carvings of images of Christ, the Virgin Mary, the disciples, and scenes from the Passion of Christ—many made in Spain and hundreds of years old—are among Colombia's most treasured works of art. Each church has at least two such works, which are either displayed or carried in processions during Holy Week.

One famous image of the Virgin Mary is *La Encarnación (The Incarnation)*;

another is *Our Lady of Sorrows*. The platforms used to carry religious statues during Holy Week processions in Popayán are covered with tortoiseshell from sea turtles caught in the Pacific Ocean.

Other religious objects dating from Spanish colonial rule also belong to the churches and are brought out during Holy Week. These include crosses, chalices, statues, and other sacred images made from gold and silver and decorated with emeralds and other jewels. Many of the religious objects were donated by wealthy families.

The churches of Popayán are fine examples of Spanish colonial architecture and are filled with beautifully carved altars and many elaborate religious paintings. Many were built during the seventeenth and eighteenth centuries and were reconstructed after the 1983 earthquake.

Music, Dance

Sacred music is most often associated with Holy Week processions in Colombia. Bands and choirs accompany the processions, setting the pace for those carrying the sacred statues. This music also helps create the Holy Week atmosphere, which also includes the tinkling of bells and the smell of burning incense.

Folk music and dancing are also part of Easter Sunday festivities. African, Indian, Caribbean, and Spanish influences blend together to make a unique traditional sound. Folk instruments are the *flauta*, a type of flute; the *marimba*, a type of xylophone; the *tiple*, a type of guitar; and the *raspa*, a percussion instrument made from a gourd. Mandolins and accordions often accompany these traditional instruments.

The *cumbia* (pronounced COOM-bee-uh) is a very popular Afro-Colombian music style. The most popular folk dances are the waltz-like *bambuco* (pronounced bom-BOO-coh) and the whirling *salsa*.

Special Role of Children, Young Adults

Children of the Puben Valley, which surrounds Popayán, have a traditional role in Holy Week processions that involves collecting candle wax. The candles used in the processions are made from the berries of laurel trees that grow on the hillsides of the Andes Mountains, near Puben. When boiled in water, the berries produce a fragrant brown and green wax. Legend says the laurel berries were given to the people by the sun as a way of lighting the darkness and keeping away fear. The candles made from this wax are called *moquitos* (pronounced moh-KEE-tohz).

After Holy Week processions, children go door to door collecting melted wax from the candles. They make their rounds in a little procession, led by one child who is called the *moquero* (pronounced moh-KAY-roh). The moquero is given melted wax to put in a little bag, but each of the other children are allowed to politely ask for any drippings from candles still burning. Boys and girls who are attracted to one another often ask for drippings from their sweethearts as tokens of friendship.

Children's processions in Popayán

Popayán holds special children's processions each day from Holy Tuesday through Good Friday of Holy Week. Children from ages five to eleven wear costumes based on their favorite characters from the adult processions. Such characters include incense bearers, university deans, archbishops, cargueros, and army colonels. The young cargueros carry small platforms with replicas of the holy figures carried by the adults. The children march along a much shorter route than the adults, but they do follow most of the town's main streets.

For More Information

Jacobsen, Peter Otto, and Preben Sejer Kristensen. *A Family in Colombia.* New York: Bookwright Press, 1986.

Markham, Lois. *Colombia: The Gateway to South America.* New York: Benchmark Books, 1997.

Perl, Lila. *Piñatas and Paper Flowers: Holidays of the Americas in English and Spanish.* New York: Clarion Books, 1983.

Web sites

"Week Santa in Popayán." [Online] http://www.ucauca.edu.co/~gacosme/popaderi.htm (accessed on February 7, 2000).

Greece

Name of Holiday: Pascha

Introduction

Easter, or Pascha (pronounced POS-kuh; Passover), is the most celebrated religious holiday in Greece and is often called the Feast of Feasts. About 98 percent of Greeks belong to the Greek Orthodox Church and participate in Holy Week observances. Shops and offices close for much of Holy Week; the holiday sometimes includes the Monday and Tuesday following Easter Sunday.

History

Historians say that Easter was well established in Greece by the second century. Religious documents written by Roman church leader Hippolytus (c. 170–c. 235) indicate that it was a nighttime ritual held on Holy Saturday. Priests read the biblical stories about the Jewish escape from slavery in Egypt, the Passover, and the death and resurrection of Jesus Christ. They chanted and lit lamps, and the bishop preached a sermon. It was also a time for baptizing those who had recently accepted Christianity and for taking Holy Communion, a ritual that involves bread and wine that has been blessed in memory of Christ's death.

Christianity became widespread in Greece through the efforts of Roman emperor Constantine the Great (ruled 306–37), who converted to Christianity in about 312. He made the great Greek city of Byzantium the capital of his Eastern Roman (Byzantine) Empire in 330, renaming it Constantinople after himself. (It is now Istanbul, Turkey). Through Constantinople, the early Greek culture developed into a new Christian civilization. Easter, then known as the Feast of Christ's Resurrection, was formally established by Emperor Constantine's Council of Nicaea (pronounced nye-SEE-uh) in 325.

Ways of celebrating Easter in Greece have changed little since the third and fourth centuries. It has remained a Saturday night vigil that features a reenactment of the death and resurrection of Jesus, beginning with his funeral procession on Good Friday. The lighting of candles as a symbol of the hope of resurrection—an Easter ritual in Eastern countries since the third century—continues to be an important part of Greek Orthodox Easter.

Folklore, Legends, Stories

Greek legends surrounding Easter are usually based on stories found in the Bible. One such legend attempts to explain why Greeks color Easter eggs in red only. According to the story, a woman was walking by carrying a basket of eggs as Christ hung on the cross. A drop of his blood fell on the eggs and stained them red. Thus began the custom of coloring eggs red in memory of the Crucifixion.

Greeks once observed very strict rules about dyeing Easter eggs. They were colored on Maundy Thursday, called Red Thursday, in a new bowl, using only a special redwood dye. The first egg to be dyed was called the "egg of the Virgin Mary" and was believed to have the power to work miracles. Certain eggs, called "evangelized eggs," were taken to church to be blessed after coloring. In some areas, people dyed one egg for each family member plus one for the Virgin Mary, the mother of Jesus. After the eggs were eaten, the shells were placed under fruit trees to help them bear fruit.

Customs, Traditions, Ceremonies

On the first Monday of Lent, called Clean Monday, many Greeks fast and eat unleavened bread, bread made without yeast. It is also a tradition to climb a mountain or high hill, or to go to the countryside and fly a kite. This may symbolize releasing desires for foods and activities that are to be given up for Lent. On Clean Monday, the sky above Mount Philopappus in the capital city of Athens is filled with multicolored kites.

The most devout Greeks fast during the forty days of Lent (*Sarakostis*) and attend church services every Friday. They fast by giving up meat, fish, eggs, and milk. They also give up wine and olive oil on Wednesdays and Fridays and during the week before Easter. Some people give up only a few of these foods; others fast only during Holy Week.

An old Greek Lenten "calendar" featured a picture of a nun who had no mouth because she could not eat certain foods for Lent. She also had seven feet, each representing one week of Lent. One foot was torn off with each passing week.

To prepare for Easter, Greek villagers give their houses, windmills, and streets a fresh coat of whitewash during Holy Week. Holy Week commemorates the Passion, or suffering, of Christ before and during his death. Early in the week, they attend more church services and read passages from the Bible, the sacred book of Christianity.

Maundy Thursday: The Crucifixion

Thursday of Holy Week, called Maundy Thursday, is marked as the eve of Christ's crucifixion. This is the first of three main Easter religious services. In the evening, the priests erect a large cross inside the church and place a large image, often wax, of Christ on the cross. They begin reading from the Bible.

Midway through the service, the priests turn out the lights and walk with a procession around the church, carrying the cross. Afterward, they again place the cross in the center of the church, and the parishioners line up to kiss it. The women and girls often stay up all night, wailing and mourning the crucified Christ. Many people also take Holy Communion to commemorate the biblical story of the Last Supper.

On Maundy Thursday, some may anoint the feet of elders or loved ones with oil made fragrant with oregano, for healing powers. This is done to commemorate an event that happened during the Last Supper: at some point during the Passover meal, Jesus washed the feet of his disciples. Holy Thursday is also the day for baking Easter bread and coloring eggs.

Good Friday: The entombment and funeral

On Good Friday, a three-hour church service ends with the Epitaphios (pronounced eh-puh-TAFF-ee-oce), or Feast of Sorrow, which is a funeral procession for the dead Christ. Many people observe a total fast on Good Friday. Some people drink vinegar or eat foods prepared with vinegar because Christ was given vinegar to drink as he suffered on the cross.

Good Friday is a government and business holiday; stores and offices are closed and flags are flown at half-mast. During the day, unmarried young women and girls, or sometimes all the village children, decorate a beautifully carved structure called the Epitaphion (pronounced eh-puh-TAFF-ee-uhn), which is covered with a gold-embroidered cloth. It is a symbol of Christ's tomb and is decorated with thousands of spring flowers sent by parish families, then strewn with rose petals and fragrant leaves.

When it is time for the church service, electric lights and candles illuminate the sanctuary. Ancient icons (religious scenes painted on wood or cloth), as well as candelabra and golden shrines, are brought out. At the end of the service, the priests remove the figure of Christ from the cross and wrap it in a funeral cloth, then carry it to the back of the church. When they return to the front of

A bishop of the Orthodox Church washes the feet of another bishop on Holy Thursday 1997, reenacting the events of the life of Jesus Christ during the days before his crucifixion. Reproduced by permission of AP/Wide World Photos.

the church, they are carrying only the cloth. This symbolizes that Christ has been entombed and only his cloth remains. The parishioners line up to kiss the symbolic tomb of Christ, decorated with thousands of flowers. Each person takes a flower from the Epitaphion in remembrance.

After dark, the congregation joins in a funeral procession in which the Epitaphion is carried through the streets. The people march slowly, each carrying a candle. A military band, playing a sad march, sometimes accompanies the procession. Church and government officials often walk behind the symbolic tomb. In some areas, people watching the procession build bonfires and burn a straw effigy, or likeness, of Judas Iscariot, the disciple who betrayed Jesus to his enemies. Women sometimes burn incense outside their front doors in honor of the passing Good Friday procession.

Holy Saturday: The Resurrection

Holy Saturday is the most joyful day in the Greek Orthodox Church, because everyone celebrates Christ's resurrection. During the day, people bake breads and cakes and either kill or purchase a lamb for Easter dinner on Sunday. Families might visit cemeteries and take food to the poor or to those who are grieving over relatives who have recently died.

Everyone gathers at the church just before 12 P.M. for midnight mass. At midnight, all lights are put out, and the priest appears carrying a flaming lantern and calling the people to "Come receive the light and glorify Christ, who is risen from the dead." Then the congregation passes the holy flame from candle to candle, until every person's candle is lit.

The priest, wearing a beautiful robe, walks out of the church with a golden cross and chants the hymn "Christ Is Risen from the Dead!" The people gather around him for a final reading from the Bible. Then he shouts, *"Christos anesti!"* (Christ is risen!), and everyone answers, *"Alithos anesti!"* (He is risen indeed!). Members of the congregation then turn to one another and exchange the Kiss of the Resurrection, or the Kiss of Love.

After the service, church bells begin to ring, ships blow their whistles in the harbor, and fireworks explode. The streets are filled with people carrying candles and shouting, *"Christos anesti!"* They carry their candles home carefully, believing it will bring good luck if the candles do not blow out. Stopping at their front door, each person blows out his candle and pinches the sooty wick. Then they draw a cross on the front door with the soot before going in.

The family breaks the Holy Week fast with an eggy soup called *mageiritsa* (pronounced mah-gay-REET-sah). After eating, they play egg games. One such game involves players trying to crack other family members' red boiled eggs with their own.

Easter Sunday: The celebration

On Easter morning, Greek people greet one another by saying, "Christ is risen!" The reply is, "He is risen indeed!" These phrases are used in greeting for the next forty days.

After the morning mass, every town holds Easter barbecue celebrations, which feature feasting on roasted lamb or goat and other foods, chanting, visiting, Greek music, and folk dancing. Villages hold community barbecues, at which ten or more lambs are roasted on spits outdoors over a bed of coals. Everyone is welcome to come and eat. Fairs are often held in conjunction with the feasts.

An old, although dangerous, Easter tradition on the Greek island of Kalymnos continues today. Men throw dynamite from the island's mountaintops to mark the beginning of the holiday and to honor those who have died at sea. The custom continues in spite of deaths and injuries caused by the explosions.

Clothing, Costumes

Everyone in Greece tries to wear at least one new article of clothing to midnight mass on Holy Saturday night, preferably new shoes. Young men often give their fiancées new shoes to wear to the Resurrection service. Most children have a new Easter outfit to wear. For the Easter Sunday celebration, folk dancers wear regional Greek costumes, with colorful vests and skirts for girls and tight knee pants for boys.

Foods, Recipes

During the Lenten fast, Greeks eat fresh vegetables, olives, fish, onions and garlic, bread, and *halvah,* a sweet made with ground sesame seeds and honey. The Lenten fast is broken with feasting that begins after midnight mass Saturday and continues throughout Easter Sunday.

Eggs for breakfast

Some people take a red boiled egg with them to midnight mass and crack and eat the egg at the end of the service. This is to show that the Lenten fast is over. They sometimes even carry salt and pepper to season their eggs. When mass is over, people shout, "Bring out the mageiritsa!" This is a soup made with egg, lemon sauce, and chicken or lamb.

Everyone goes home after mass to a breakfast feast that might also include a lemony chicken and rice soup called *avogolemono* and a cheese pie called *tiropita.* Red-colored eggs are brought out as sym-

Melopitta (Easter Honey Pie)

Ingredients

½ cup sugar

2 cups cottage cheese

½ cup cream cheese, softened at room temperature

1 cup honey

1 teaspoon almond extract

4 eggs, lightly beaten

½ cup coarsely chopped almonds or other nuts

1 single pie crust, thawed if frozen

cinnamon for sprinkling

Directions

1. Blend together sugar, cottage cheese, and cream cheese, then add honey, almond extract, and eggs, blending constantly.

2. Stir in nuts, and then pour mixture into pie crust.

3. Bake at 350 degrees for about 45 minutes, or until crust is golden brown and pie is firm.

4. Remove from oven and sprinkle with cinnamon. Serve at room temperature.

bols of the blood of Christ. People drink Greek wine called *retsina* with this meal.

Roasting the "Passover lamb"

On Easter morning, people prepare cooking fires to roast a whole lamb or goat. In rural areas, people dig a shallow trench and fill it with charcoal, then set a spit over the trench. The lamb is roasted for hours, with people taking turns rotating the spit by hand. The meat is seasoned with wild oregano and basted with lemon juice and olive oil.

Popular appetizers for the Easter Sunday feast are a cucumber-yogurt dip and stuffed grape leaves. Other popular foods are *spanakopita* (pronounced spah-nuh-KOH-pee-tuh), pastry filled with spinach and feta cheese; roast chicken; roasted potatoes seasoned with lemon juice, or sometimes French fries; green beans; orzo, rice-shaped pasta; lamb sausage; and an Easter bread called the Bread of Christ or *lambropsoma* (pronounced lahm-brop-SOH-muh), made with whole red-dyed eggs in the center and a cross shape cut into the crust.

Greek Easter desserts

For dessert, butter cookies are popular, along with Easter cookies baked in shapes of religious symbols. Greek women on the island of Cyprus prepare cheese pastries called *flaounas,* on Good Friday, competing to see who has the best recipe. Flaky cream-filled pastries, halvah, and *tsoureki* (pronounced soo-REH-kee) cake are other popular Easter desserts. Tsoureki cake is an Easter bread that contains lots of eggs and is shaped into loaves or braided.

Arts, Crafts, Games

The religious paintings, called icons, that are displayed in Greek Orthodox churches were painted as long ago as the Byzantine period (fourth through seventh centuries). They continued to be created through the late 1500s.

These works of art were sometimes painted directly onto wooden panels. They may also have been painted on linen or cotton cloth, or occasionally on parchment, that was glued to wooden panels. They depict figures and events associated with Jesus' last days and may include Jesus on the cross, Jesus' mother Mary weeping at his feet, and the Last Supper. The icons are hung where they can easily be seen; some people pray before them and kiss them. Many Greeks have small copies of the icons in their homes.

Palms grow in southern Greece, and palm fronds have been used since at least the ninth century to decorate churches, inside and out, on Palm Sunday. The fronds are braided into little baskets, crosses, and stars. Bay and myrtle are used in the north, where palms do not grow.

After church services on Palm Sunday, priests traditionally present each member of the congregation with a *vaya,* a bay or myrtle sprig with a little cross made from a palm frond. After the Palm Sunday service, people take their vayas home and touch things they wish to bless with them, including animals and crops. The vayas are then tucked inside the frames of religious paintings, where they are said to protect the household from danger and sickness.

Red Easter eggs

On Thursday of Holy Week, people prepare *kokina avga* (red-dyed eggs) for Easter. They are boiled and then dyed red, symbolizing the blood of Christ and his sacrifice for mankind. A traditional red dye used is cochineal, made from the bodies of small female cochineal insects.

After the eggs are dyed, they are wiped with olive oil to make them shine. They are displayed on a plate or used to decorate the tsoureki cake. In some areas, people draw designs on the eggs, using a needle dipped in melted wax. These are called "embroidered" or "partridge" eggs.

Decorating the church and *lambades*

On Saturday night before Easter, churches are decorated with strings of lights, greenery, and blue and white Greek flags. Sprigs of rosemary, called the herb of remembrance, are often strewn over the floor, giving the church a pungent evergreen scent. People carry *lambades* (pronounced lom-BAH-dehs), or candles, with ribbons tied around them. Godparents buy children special lambades decorated with white or blue ribbons, gold thread, and flowers.

Egg fights and games

Many Greeks and Greek Americans play an egg-fighting game on Easter in which two people each hold a boiled colored egg, vertically, one over top of the other. The person on top uses one end of his or her egg to tap one end of the bottom egg. After all eggs have been fought, the person who comes away with an uncracked egg wins. In another traditional Greek Easter game, an egg hangs from the ceiling on a string. A player starts the egg swinging by bopping it with his head. He then tries to catch the egg in his mouth.

Music, Dance

Lenten services in Greek Orthodox churches include all-male choirs chanting the classical hymn "Kyrie Eleison" ("Lord, Have Mercy"). Hymns about the Passion of Christ are sung during the Maundy Thurs-day evening service. As the women and girls mourn the death of Jesus, they sing "The Virgin's Lament." After the Saturday night Resurrection service, priests chant the hymn "Christ Is Risen from the Dead."

Easter Sunday afternoon is filled with folk dancing and folk music played on the *bouzouki* (a mandolin-like instrument), the fiddle, the accordion, and the *santouri,* a Greek dulcimer.

Special Role of Children, Young Adults

Children and young adults have important roles in Easter season church services, including decorating the Epitaphion with flowers for the Good Friday procession. Children may gather firewood for bonfires used to burn an effigy of Judas Iscariot on Good Friday. They help color Easter eggs and bake breads and cakes, help decorate the church, and carry specially decorated candles to midnight mass on Holy Saturday and on Easter Sunday. They may perform traditional Greek folk dances on Easter Sunday. Although Greek Orthodox Easter is not a day for the Easter bunny and Easter baskets as in some countries, children get new outfits and sometimes receive chocolate eggs and little Easter gifts.

For More Information

DuBois, Jill. *Greece.* New York: Marshall Cavendish, 1993.

Spyropulos, Diana. *Greece: A Spirited Independence.* Minneapolis: Dillon, 1990.

Web sites

"The Passions of Christ: A Journey through Byzantine Art." [Online] http://www.hol.gr/greece/events/

easter/byzantine (accessed on February 4, 2000).

Van Haas, Gary. "Greek Easter Holy Week." [Online] http://www.gogreece.com/learn/easter.htm (accessed on February 7, 2000).

Poland

Name of Holiday: Wielkanoc

Introduction

Easter, or Wielkanoc (pronounced vyel-KAH-nots), is the most important religious holiday of the year for people living in Poland, about 90 percent of whom are Roman Catholic. Poles are deeply religious, and their faith has sustained them as a people through centuries of difficult times. They mark the death and Resurrection of Jesus Christ with special masses, processions and Passion plays, and a magnificent Easter Sunday breakfast feast.

History

During the tenth century, Poland adopted Christianity when Prince Mieszko (pronounced MYESH-kaw) I was baptized at Easter in 966. Prince Mieszko is considered the founder of the Polish state and its first great leader. He is credited with setting Poland on the path of development it would follow for centuries.

In more modern times, the Polish people have endured a long history of uprising and defeat, death, exile, and destruction of their state. At one time, Poland claimed land stretching from the Oder River in Germany to the Dnieper River in Russia and from the Black Sea in the south to the Baltic Sea in the north. Its neighbors gradually chipped away at the country's territory until, by 1795, when Poland was dismembered and divided among Russia, Prussia, and Austria, it ceased to exist on the maps of the world.

Throughout these difficult times, the Catholic Church served as the primary source of hope and moral guidance for the Polish people. Nowhere is that influence more evident than in the church's Easter celebrations, which have for centuries helped the people maintain some of their most cherished traditions. During the early 1980s, for example, when the Polish people fought back against the Soviet Communist government with the Solidarity (unity) movement, the Catholic Church sheltered Polish citizens and provided meeting places for those organizing demonstrations.

In Warsaw and other cities, Poles continued to observe Easter openly and passionately. People still carried their Easter baskets to church to be blessed. Many decorated their baskets with Solidarity pins. With the coming of democratic government in 1989, the Polish people have joyously renewed all their religious celebrations and customs.

Folklore, Legends, Stories

One of Poland's most holy sites is the shrine of the Virgin Mary located in the Monastery of the Pauline Fathers at Jasna Gora (pronounced YAHZ-nuh GOO-ruh; Mount of Light) in the town of Czestochowa (pronounced chent-stuh-KOH-vuh). It is here that Poland's most famous religious icon, the Black Madonna, is housed. The icon is called the "Black" Madonna because the painting has darkened with age and from centuries of soot from candles left burning to illuminate the painting for visitors.

According to religious legend, the Black Madonna—which depicts the Virgin Mary holding the infant Jesus—was painted by Saint Luke, follower of Christ and author of the biblical New Testament Gospel of Saint Luke. It is said that Mary talked with Saint Luke as he painted her portrait, telling him the story of Jesus' birth and life. Luke later recorded the stories in the Bible.

The icon is painted on a piece of cypress wood that supposedly was a table-top taken from a table built by Jesus, who learned the carpenter's trade from his father, Joseph. Another legend says the table was built by Joseph.

The Virgin Mary, through the Black Madonna, is believed to have protected nations under siege since the fourth century. She is said to have saved the Eastern Roman city of Constantinople when the painting was displayed from the city's walls.

The icon passed from owner to owner until the late 1300s, when Prince Ladislaus II (pronounced LAH-dee-sloss) of Poland (ruled 1386–1434) placed it in a church in Czestochowa. He later had the Pauline monastery built to more safely house the painting. In 1430, according to legend, a Hussite soldier fell down dead after striking the painting twice with his sword. The markings can still be seen on the painting.

The Virgin Mary is credited with saving Poland from being taken over by Swedish armies in 1655. During this battle, only the area around the monastery at Czestochowa remained unconquered in all of Poland. By a miracle, the monks were able to hold off the Swedes for forty days, and Poland was eventually able to drive the armies out. The Swedish soldiers claimed to have seen the figure of Mary in the sky over the monastery, protecting it with her blue cloak. They also said bullets they fired at the monastery seemed to bounce back at them.

After the Swedish forces withdrew from the monastery, the king of Poland placed his nation under the protection of the Virgin Mary, or Bogurodzica (pronounced bah-guh-rahd-ZEE-cuh; the Mother of God), as she is called in Poland. In 1920, the Virgin is said to have again appeared as a vision in the sky as Russian soldiers prepared to attack Warsaw, Poland's capital. The soldiers disbanded and fled.

Over the years, thousands of people have made pilgrimages to see the Black Madonna, and miraculous cures have been reported for centuries. The number of pilgrimages greatly increased when Poland became a free nation in 1989. Some 100,000 people make a pilgrimage to Jasna Gora each year to renew their vows to the Mother of God and to leave tokens of gratitude for healing miracles. Special Holy Thursday services at the monastery include changing the vestments (garment-like coverings) of the painting.

Easter egg legends and Easter lore

There are many legends about the origin of painted Polish Easter eggs, called *pysanky*. One says the biblical Mary Magdalene and other followers of Christ took sweet spices in a basket to Christ's tomb to wash his body. They also carried along some boiled eggs to eat later. When they arrived at the tomb, they found the eggs had been colored with many beautiful patterns. Another story says Mary, the mother of Christ, painted boiled eggs and showed them to the baby Jesus as he lay in his cradle.

Pysanky are said to protect the house from evil, fire, and storm. An old custom is to bury a few pysanky in the ground to protect grapevines and other crops against bad weather. Farmers also rubbed their animals with raw egg to ensure fertility. After Easter Sunday, they rubbed the animals with fat from Easter meats to guarantee good health.

Families believed that having priests bless baskets of food carried to church on Holy Saturday would ensure plenty of food for the coming year. Because they wanted to use every bit of the blessed Easter food, farmers ground eggshells and planted them in their fields, in each of the four directions. They chanted, "Some for the mice, some for the birds, some for the worms, and some for the animals of the forest, so they might leave the crops alone." Children threw colored eggshells into streams, believing the shells would reach gnomes living underground and tell them spring had come.

People once believed that swallowing the tip of a pussy willow sprig used in Palm Sunday mass would cure a sore throat and bring good health. They also stuck a few sprigs into molehills to drive away the moles and protect crops. People gently slapped one another with pussy willows on Palm Sunday to ensure fertile farmland and many children. They also placed the willows behind religious icons for protection from fire, storms, and evil spirits.

Customs, Traditions, Ceremonies

Poles strictly observe the forty-day fast of Lent in order to prepare their bodies and minds for the year's greatest religious feast at Easter. Families go to church all week during Holy Week and also clean houses, barns, and yards to spruce them up for the holidays. Spring fairs are held during Holy Week, and farmers come into town with the season's first vegetables and livestock to sell.

Holy Week processions and Passion plays

In Poland, Palm Sunday is called "Flower Sunday." Pussy willow or raspberry branches decorated with ribbons—representing palms—are carried in processions to and from churches. Pussy willows that have been blessed by a priest are placed in water after Palm Sunday processions, and they flower by Easter Sunday.

The small town of Kalwaria Zebrzydowska has the most well-known palm processions. It is also home to Poland's most famous Passion plays. The plays are held at a monastery on the side of a hill and are viewed by thousands of people each year. Local villagers are tied to crosses, and a man dressed as Jesus Christ carries a crucifix. Villagers and religious pilgrims dress as Romans, Pharisees (members of an ancient Jewish group), and Christ's disciples. Artificial palm branches are made for the processions by local artisans. They can reach up to thirty feet long and are beautifully decorated with flowers and ribbons.

An elaborate Holy Thursday procession involves an effigy, or likeness, of Judas Iscariot, the disciple who betrayed Jesus.

"Judas" is flogged and dragged out of town, then hanged, drowned, or burned. Church bells stop ringing on the morning of Holy Thursday; parents tell their children that the bells have all gone to Rome, home of the pope, who is head of the Roman Catholic Church. It was also tradition for people to build fires in different parts of town and invite the poor to come and warm themselves and eat food brought by each family. Holy Thursday is also the day when many women do their Easter baking.

Visiting the "tombs"

On Good Friday, people visit artificial "tombs" of Christ. These are cavelike structures that are built at churches for Easter each year, although some are solidly constructed and stand year round. A replica of Christ's body is placed in each tomb and covered with flowers. Devout Catholics keep a vigil at the tombs throughout the day and night.

Good Friday is considered a day of mourning; people do not bathe, bake bread, or slaughter animals for meat. Some Poles cover their mirrors with a black veil on Good Friday to remember they are in mourning for Christ. It is also a day of strict fasting—many neither eat nor drink. Polish tradition calls for a fast from Good Friday until Easter Sunday. During this time, no hot food is to be served, and many people eat only bread and cold roasted potatoes. Good Friday is the day when many women and children color hard-boiled eggs and decorate pysanky.

Blessing the Easter foods

On Holy Saturday, baskets of Easter foods, or "blessing baskets," are taken to church to be blessed. These foods, called "hallow (holy) fare," include ham, sausages, Easter bread called *babka* (pronounced BOB-kuh; grandmother), rye bread, Easter cheese, butter, salt, horseradish, small sugar lambs, and decorated eggs, called pysanky. As in Ukraine, families often cover their baskets with beautifully embroidered handmade cloths.

At church, the priest blesses the baskets by sprinkling them with holy water. In smaller villages, the Easter foods are laid out on each family's table, and the priest visits the various households to bless the food. After the baskets are blessed, the Lenten fast is considered to be over. The blessed foods are eaten on Easter Sunday morning during a big, festive breakfast.

Some Poles keep an old custom called "the blessing of fire and water." They put out the old fire in the hearth and relight it with a candle from church. In addition to having baskets of food blessed, they also bring containers of water to church to be blessed. The containers are then kept at home as protection for crops and animals.

On Holy Saturday Eve, villagers march to church in Resurrection processions. A candlelight Resurrection service is held, with a figure of the risen Christ placed on the church altar. At the end of the service, members of some congregations march around the church three times, an old tradition. Guns were once fired to celebrate the Resurrection.

Easter Sunday festivities

The Polish Easter Sunday greeting is "A joyful Alleluia to you!" This greeting has been used for hundreds of years. The church bells are said to "fly back from

Rome" on Easter morning, and to once again ring joyfully. Some people keep the tradition of giving one another an Easter kiss after the Easter mass.

After mass, people go home to Easter Sunday breakfast, which is equal to Christmas dinner in importance. The table is set with the family's very best linens and china. Every family member is served a piece of a blessed boiled egg with salt and pepper and a piece of Easter bread spread with horseradish for protection against sickness in the coming year. Family members wish one another good health and happiness.

Smigus-Dyngus water fights

On the day after Easter, called "Dyngus," in a custom similar to that in Ukraine, men and boys spray women and girls with water. On Tuesday, the girls and women take their revenge and drench the men and boys. This tradition is called "Smigus-Dyngus" (pronounced SHMEE-goose DEEN-goose).

Boys once made primitive water guns using hollow wooden sticks filled with water that they pushed out with a wooden rod. In some areas, boys douse girls with perfume and receive a small gift in return. In cities, Smigus-Dyngus is usually practiced only by children.

The origins of Smigus-Dyngus are many. First, the custom is thought to stem from the ancient belief that water is the source of all life. It is also considered to be a celebration of spring and Christ's resurrection. Finally, it is said to commemorate the group baptisms that were conducted during the tenth century, when the Polish people first adopted Christianity.

Clothing, Costumes

Polish people once believed they must wear at least one new article of clothing on Good Friday or they would have only worn-out clothes to wear for the rest of the year. Today, most Polish people dress in conservative Western-style clothing, but traditional Polish folk costumes are worn on Easter Sunday. Women wear multicolored lace skirts and aprons, hats and bonnets, and embroidered bodices and vests. Men's shirts, tunics, and pants are also embroidered with traditional designs. Red and white, Poland's national colors, are favorite colors of the season.

Foods, Recipes

Postna zupa (Lenten soup) is a vegetable broth eaten during Lent, when Poles maintain a fast in preparation for the Feast of the Resurrection at Easter. Lenten soup is made with carrots, celery, onion, and parsley sauteed in butter and simmered in water. The vegetable pieces are strained out before the broth is served.

Because eggs are not eaten during the fast of Lent, farming households have always saved eggs produced during this time to use for pysanky and other colored eggs. There are plenty of eggs to give away and plenty left for the household to cook with and eat. Many traditional Easter foods contain lots of eggs.

The Easter breakfast table

Poland is known for its big Easter feast, perhaps the most elaborate of all countries celebrating Easter. The table is decorated with foliage, flowers, and pysanky and set with the finest china,

A Polish youth chases a young woman with a bucket of water on Easter Monday in Warsaw in 1999. It is a tradition for men and boys to spray women and girls with water on Dyngus, the day after Easter. Reproduced by permission of AP/Wide World Photos.

linens, and silver. A lamb, representing Christ, is the centerpiece. It is either molded from a sugar mixture or baked as a bread or cake. A sacred flag may be placed on top.

Feast of feasts

The family will feast on big platters of meats such as ham, roast pork, veal, turkey, goose, and Polish *kielbasa* (sausage) with sauerkraut. Side dishes include salads, stuffed cabbage, boiled eggs, cold beet and cucumber soup, and cucumbers in sour cream. Vinegar will be on the table as a reminder of the vinegar Christ was given to drink as he suffered on the cross.

A large loaf of Easter bread, called babka, is made from yeast dough and raisins and flavored with lemon and orange rind. Family babka recipes are passed down for generations. Other breads on the Easter breakfast table are braided Polish love knots called *chrusciki*. Butter molded into the shape of a lamb is placed near the breads.

Polish cooks make little marzipan (a paste made from sugar, almond paste, and

Polish Easter Cheese

Ingredients

1 quart milk

1 teaspoon salt

1 tablespoon sugar

1 dozen eggs, beaten

Directions

1. Heat milk to steaming, then add eggs, sugar, and salt. Simmer on very low, stirring with a wooden spoon.

2. When the mixture has separated into solids and water, strain it through cheesecloth.

3. Tie up the top of the cloth to make a bag and press the cheese into a ball. Hang the bag up to drain.

4. When the cheese is completely cool and has stopped dripping, remove it from the cheesecloth and refrigerate. Slice the cheese to eat with bread or use it to make cheesecake.

egg whites) models of each food prepared for the Easter feast. These are placed on the table on an elegant china plate. Horseradish is a traditional Polish Easter food, and *cwikla* (pronounced TSVIK-lah), a relish made from horseradish mixed with beets, is usually on the Easter table.

For dessert

Huge cakes called *baby* (pronounced BOB-ee) are an Easter favorite. They can be plain or layered and may be flavored with vanilla, chocolate, almond, lemon, saffron, orange, figs, or other ingredients. Poppyseed cakes and a flat cake topped with nut paste and cheese, called *mazurek* (pronounced mah-ZOO-rek) are also served at Easter breakfast. Mazurek is iced and decorated with jams, nuts, and raisins and may also be decorated with marzipan pussy willow branches, chocolate flowers, and icing letters that say "Alleluia."

Traditional cheesecake made with homemade Easter cheese is one of the most traditional Polish Easter foods. Easter cheese is one of the foods included in the "blessing baskets" taken to church on Holy Saturday. Spiced, sweetened vodka called *krupnik* is served to the adults with dessert.

After Easter Sunday, leftover meats are made into the Polish national dish, *bigos,* or hunter's stew, a hearty main dish that can contain five or six different meats.

Arts, Crafts, Games

Easter egg decorating is an art in Poland, as it is in Ukraine. There are four different types of egg decorating in Poland. Boiled eggs dyed a single color are called *malowanki.* Malowanki with patterns etched into them with a sharp instrument are called *skrobanki.* Pysanky are created using the shells of raw eggs, with the yolk and white blown out after tapping tiny holes in the top and bottom of the egg. Polish women and girls use a wax method, as in Ukraine, to create geometrical or abstract patterns and Christian symbols like the fish and the cross. Some paint flowers and other designs on the eggs instead of using the wax method.

A fourth way Polish women and girls make pysanky is by cutting intricate designs from paper or fabric and gluing them onto the eggshells. This same paper-cutting technique is used to make large cut-paper designs called *wycinanki,* a popular Polish folk art.

Pysanky are given as Easter gifts to friends and godparents, but not usually to immediate family members. A girl will often give pysanky or skrobanki to a young man whom she would like to have for a boyfriend. People of Polish heritage living in other countries continue the pysanky-making tradition and keep Polish Easter customs as faithfully as possible.

Music, Dance

On Easter Sunday, Polish girls often perform traditional group folk dances and sing folk songs. Polish folk music is played on instruments such as the fiddle, single-reed bagpipe, pan pipes, and accordion. Village folk musicians often entertain at Easter and at other festivals during the year. The polka and the mazurka are favorite forms of Polish folk dancing.

Special Role of Children, Young Adults

Polish children attend church faithfully with their parents during Holy Week. Girls help with Easter baking and coloring Easter eggs. They learn the art of making pysanky from their mothers. Parents sometimes wake their children on Good Friday by tapping them gently with branches or sticks, as a reminder that this is the day Christ died on the cross.

On Easter Sunday, some children receive chocolate lambs or Easter eggs as treats. Children love spraying one another with water on Easter Monday and often sing-song the name of this activity, making it rhyme by chanting, "Shmingus-Dingus" instead of "Smigus-Dyngus."

For More Information

Heale, Jay. *Poland.* New York: Marshall Cavendish, 1994.

Pfeiffer, Christine. *Poland: Land of Freedom Fighters.* Minneapolis: Dillon, 1991.

Web sites

"Easter." [Online] http://members.tripod.com/temperka85/easter.html (accessed on February 4, 2000).

McCann, Judy. "Memories of a Polish Easter." [Online] http://www.foodwine.com/destinations/poland/poleaster.html (accessed on February 4, 2000).

Spain

Name of Holiday: Semana Santa

Introduction

Easter and Holy Week (Semana Santa; pronounced say-MAH-nuh SAHN-tuh) celebrations in Spain are among the most outstanding and passionate in the world. Although Easter is the most sacred holiday season of the year and is observed with extreme reverence, it is also a very colorful and boisterous holiday marked by thousands of parades and *fiestas,* or parties. From Palm Sunday through Easter Sunday, cities and towns all over Spain are a riot of color, emotion, and celebration as people fervently commemorate Jesus Christ's death and resurrection.

History

The earliest known accounts of Holy Week celebrations come from a woman named Egeria, believed to have been a nun from northern Spain. In 381, Egeria began a three-year pilgrimage to Christian holy sites. She wrote down detailed observations about Holy Week observances in Egypt, Jerusalem and Palestine, and Asia Minor (modern-day Turkey).

By the time of Egeria's journey, the Holy Land had become a major destination for Christian pilgrims. Worshipers moved from one holy site to the next, listening to readings from the Bible, the sacred book of Christianity, and recalling events from the life of Christ. The locations in Jerusalem that marked the events leading up to Christ's crucifixion and resurrection and the commemoration of these events became known as the stations of the cross.

The pilgrims, including Egeria, took their reports of Holy Week observances in the Holy Land home with them. Word of their observances quickly spread and people throughout the Christian world adopted many of the religious practices. Soon after Egeria's pilgrimage, Spain held the first reported Easter procession in the Western Church. The procession took place on Palm Sunday. By the seventh century, Holy Week observances had spread to present-day France and England.

Over the next centuries, Holy Week commemorations in Spain and the rest of Europe evolved as the laws of church and state changed. In Spain, as elsewhere, the celebrations and traditions were influenced by the various cultures of each region.

Most current Holy Week traditions in Spain began during the sixteenth century. One tradition involved helping members of the church better understand the Easter story. Prior to this time, traditional ceremonies and masses were said in Latin, a language that was not spoken by the majority of people. The Church commissioned famous artists to create life-size images of the biblical figures from Christ's Passion (suffering) and resurrection. The figures were then paraded through the streets at Easter. These processions brought the biblical story to life and started a tradition that has remained at the heart of Holy Week celebrations in Spain to this day.

Folklore, Legends, Stories

Religious legends abound during this most holy time of year in Spain. The legend of the Holy Grail is among the most popular. Old folk customs surrounding Lent add a note of humor to the season.

The Holy Grail and the cathedral of Saint James

The cup that, according to medieval legend, was used by Jesus at the Last Supper is housed at the cathedral in Valencia, Spain. Called the Santo Grial, or Holy Grail, it is made of agate and embellished with twenty-six pearls, two emeralds, and two rubies. It is said to have belonged to the Virgin Mary, who visited Spain to see James, one of Jesus' disciples. Later known as Saint James, he was one of the first to preach Christianity in Spain.

Saint James is considered the patron saint of Spain. His grave is said to rest beneath the cathedral of Santiago de Compostela (Saint James of Compostela), in Galicia. Built in the twelfth century, it is Spain's holiest shrine and one of the most visited shrines in Europe.

The seven-legged woman

An old Spanish folk custom was to make a cardboard figure of a woman with seven legs, with each leg representing the seven weeks of Lent. Each week, the figure was carried through town and one of its legs was pulled off. During the final week of Lent, Passion Week, the figure was burned on a bonfire.

Customs, Traditions, Ceremonies

Palm Sunday is called Pascua Florida, or "Flowery Easter." (The Spanish explorer Ponce de León gave the state of Florida its name because he discovered the flowery territory on Easter Sunday in 1513.) Palm fronds are blessed, then taken home and placed on balconies as lightning rods throughout the year, following an old tradition. Many of the palm fronds, some as long as six feet, are cut from a palm forest at Elche, on the southern Mediterranean coast of Spain.

Holy Week processions

During Holy Week, more than three thousand processions depicting scenes surrounding the death and resurrection of Christ are held throughout Spain. The most spectacular and well-known processions take place in the city of Seville, where from four to eight processions are held simultaneously each day from Palm Sunday through Easter Sunday. Because of the large number of processions held on Holy Thursday and Good Friday, city streets are closed to auto traffic. Pilgrims from all over the world throng at the foot of Seville's cathedral, the second largest in Europe, to watch the parades.

The processions have remained almost unchanged since the sixteenth century, thanks to the Catholic Church, which adheres strictly to tradition and ceremony. They are similar throughout the country but are stamped with each region's own character or accent.

Leading the Holy Week processions are *nazarenos* (pronounced nah-zuh-RAY-nohs), men who dress in long white gowns with tall, white, pointed hoods that cover their heads, faces, and shoulders. These robes are called *capuchones* (pronounced cah-poo-CHOH-nays). Some nazarenos carry large wooden crosses to repent for wrongs they have done. Others carry six-foot-tall candles and chant prayers. In Murcia, Spain, the nazarenos carry candies and pastries under their robes, making their stomachs look fat. They lose the "weight" as the procession continues because they throw all their candy to the children in the crowd.

Heavy parade floats called *pasos* carry life-size wooden sculptures depicting such biblical scenes as the Last Supper of Jesus and his disciples, Christ bearing the cross he would be crucified on, Christ at the Crucifixion in custody of the Roman soldiers, and the Virgin Mary, the mother of Jesus. Figures of Mary are often dressed in elaborate gowns and wear glittering jewels. They are sometimes fitted with real hair and eyebrows and shed glass tears. The pasos

Hooded nazarenos, penitents mourning the death of Jesus Christ, lead the Good Friday procession through the streets of Segovia, Spain, in 1999. Many Holy Week processions have remained almost unchanged since the sixteenth century. Reproduced by permission of AP/Wide World Photos.

glow with thousands of candles held in silver holders and are adorned with beautiful flowers. Crowds line the streets to watch as the candlelit images parade through darkened streets to the beat of a single drum.

The images are escorted by members of *cofradías* (pronounced koh-frah-DEE-uhs), ancient religious brotherhoods. They wear long, brightly colored robes and tall, pointed hoods with slits cut in them so they can see. Seville area brotherhoods have more than one hundred pasos, which they store in the fifty-eight local cathedrals and churches between processions.

Some twenty-five to forty men, known as *costaleros* (pronounced cos-tuh-LAY-rohs), carry the heavy floats on their shoulders, using rolled-up sacks called *costals* as padding. For one float, forty-two men carry 142 pounds each. The crowd cannot see the costaleros, because they walk underneath the floats, which have long skirting draped from the edges.

A leader walks before each float to let the carriers know when to start and stop. As the floats move along, they sway gently with the movements of the costaleros, making the wooden figures seem almost lifelike.

Occasionally, a high-pitched wail, or *saeta* (arrow), an improvised song of grief sung by a spectator, pierces the air and the procession comes to a halt, giving the costaleros a chance to rest.

Many of the paso images were carved during the seventeenth century. *La Macarena,* the Virgin of Good Hope, is the best-loved. She belongs to the brotherhood of bullfighters and gypsies. She has a scar on her left cheek inflicted when an intoxicated man in the crowd threw his wineglass at her. To atone for his deed, he walked in chains among the nazarenos for eight years during Holy Week. *La Macarena* is borne on an elaborate float laden with a multitude of flowers and hundreds of candles. Before she is returned to her place at the cathedral on Good Friday night, the men carrying her float rock it from side to side to make the Virgin "dance."

In the city of Lorca, two regional groups compete to see which has the most elaborately decorated statue of the Virgin Mary. One is the Virgin of Suffering, or the Blue Virgin, and the other is the Virgin of Bitterness, or the White Virgin. The groups spend large amounts of money on adornments for the statues and on the processions themselves, which include some two hundred Spanish stallions.

The penitents

As do people in the Philippines and some other countries, some Spaniards perform extreme acts of penitence (repenting of sins) at Easter. Called *picaos* (pronounced pee-KYE-ohs), the barebacked penitents whip themselves with cloth or leather whips as they pass by the stations of the Passion.

Others are bound tightly to makeshift crosses with ropes.

Lighting the Paschal candle

Masses are held throughout Holy Week in Spain, but a highlight of these services is the lighting of the huge Paschal candle, which in some cathedrals can weigh up to eight hundred pounds. The candle is lit on the morning of Holy Saturday in anticipation of Christ's resurrection. Throughout Lent and Holy Week, it is concealed behind a purple veil that also hides the church altar. The veil is drawn on Holy Saturday as people kneel to pray. Holy Saturday is also the day that church bells resume ringing. During Holy Week, no bells are rung in Spain from Holy Thursday until Easter Saturday.

Burning Judas

In some parts of Spain, including Andalusia and the Basque country, people make a life-size straw or rag effigy (representation) of Judas Iscariot during Holy Week. According to the Bible, Judas was the disciple who betrayed Jesus for thirty pieces of silver. The straw man is suspended by a rope over the street and is burned on Easter Sunday or Monday. "Judas" is sometimes filled with rockets or other fireworks, which adds a spectacular effect when he is set on fire. In the town of Alonso, riflemen use an effigy of Judas as a target during "Judas' Party." The children drag the remains through the town streets.

Dances, fairs, and bullfights

On Easter Sunday afternoon, there is dancing and people go to bullfights. On Easter Monday, large fairs open in many Spanish cities. These are filled with music and dancing, feasting and drinking, trading cattle, buying and selling crafts, and showing off gorgeous folk costumes.

Battle of Flowers

In the city of Murcia, people welcome spring with the Bando de la Huerta (Battle of Flowers), which begins on Easter Monday and lasts about two weeks. This colorful festival includes music, dancing, processions, fireworks, speeches, and a parade in which groups compete to see which one has the most colorful, blossom-bedecked float.

Clothing, Costumes

On Easter Saturday in Spain, women discard the black lace mourning clothes they have worn since Good Friday night. On Easter Sunday and during the fiestas and bullfights that begin on Monday, they dress in festive folk costumes or simply wear the Western-style clothing that is the norm in most cities. The carved wooden Passion figures featured on pasos, or floats, are dressed in real costumes, often expensive robes embroidered with gold and studded with jewels.

Foods, Recipes

On Easter Saturday, families begin preparing for the Easter Sunday feast. As in other Mediterranean countries, roast lamb is often the main Easter dish. Good wines are also chosen.

A Spanish Easter bread decorated with red-dyed eggs is made, similar to the Easter bread made in Greece. It is called *monja*, meaning "nun," and is baked in a round loaf. The top is marked with a cross, with red eggs at the four corners of the cross, making a beautiful decoration for the Easter table.

A famous traditional Easter sweet made in Toledo, Spain, is *mazapán* (marzipan), made from almond paste, sugar, and egg and formed into intricate religious shapes. Sweets served at fiestas on Easter Sunday include *turrón* (a chocolate nougat) and *yemas,* made from egg yolks boiled with syrup.

Spain's national dish is *paella* (pronounced pie-A-yuh), made with seafood, chicken, and rice. It is traditionally served at both Easter and Christmas in a large oven-proof skillet called a *paellera.*

Arts, Crafts, Games

Figures that are displayed on pasos during Holy Week processions are considered treasured works of art in Spain. Many were originally carved from wood by famous Spanish artists and sculptors. One of the finest figures featured in Seville's Easter celebrations is called the *Agony in the Garden,* which was built by sculptor Francisco Salzillo (1707–1783). According to legend, Salzillo carved the figures from a drawing furnished by an angel whom Salzillo had given a room for the night.

Another favorite image in Seville is a figure of Christ that was carved during the seventeenth century by sculptor Juan de Mesa. As the image is carried in Holy Week processions, it draws many kinds of emotions from the onlookers. Some people cry, some laugh, some confess their sins, and many reach out to touch the famous image.

Spanish Easter Paella

Ingredients

12 mussels or clams (or 6 of each), scrubbed

3 pounds chicken, cut into bite-size pieces

2 cups lobster meat, cut into chunks

1 pound washed, peeled, deveined shrimp

2 Italian sausages (or 2 chorizo), sliced

2 cups chopped ham

1 teaspoon dried saffron, or 1 teaspoon ground turmeric

2 cups rice

1 can stewed tomatoes, drained and chopped

1 cup green beans

1 cup peas

1 bell pepper, chopped

1 large onion, chopped

3 cloves garlic, diced

1 large bay leaf

2 tablespoons chopped fresh Italian parsley

about ½ cup olive oil

4 cups chicken broth

salt and pepper to taste

Directions

1. Heat broth and add saffron or turmeric.

2. In large Dutch oven or *paellera,* fry chicken pieces in 2 tablespoons of oil until browned. Sprinkle with a little salt and pepper, remove from Dutch oven, and set aside.

3. Add 2 more tablespoons of oil to Dutch oven and fry onions, garlic, bell pepper, and sausage pieces until sausage is browned. Remove sausage and set aside.

4. Preheat oven to 450 degrees. Add chicken broth and bay leaf to Dutch oven and bring to a boil.

5. Add rice, tomatoes, peas, and green beans, bring to a boil again, season with salt and pepper, then remove from heat.

6. Add shrimp, lobster, and ham, stirring well to mix. Bury mussels or clams in the rice mixture, cover, and simmer for 15 minutes. Throw away any mussels or clams with shells that did not open.

7. Place chicken pieces and sausage on top of rice mixture, cover, and bake in preheated oven for 15 minutes.

8. Stir chicken and sausage into paella and garnish with parsley. Serve piping hot, right from the Dutch oven.

The Spanish Easter egg town

Although Easter eggs are not common in much of Spain, they have a special place in the town of Pola de Siero. Two months before Easter, people in Polo de Siero begin preparing the eggs. First, they clean the eggs thoroughly with soap. Then they draw designs either directly on the eggs or on tracing paper so the designs can be transferred to the eggs. Next, the eggs are cooked and dyed, and the designs—which include names, animals, poems, and flowers—are painted.

The decorated eggs are given to friends or sold to tourists from all over Spain during an Easter Tuesday fiesta. For the fiesta, there is a parade, with children and adults dressed in native costumes. The streets are decorated with tree branches tied with wire, and large barrels of cider line the parade route to take care of the thirsty.

Easter chocolate

In other parts of Spain, elaborately decorated chocolate Easter eggs are popular. The eggs are placed in baskets decorated with stuffed animals such as rabbits or chicks and given to children as gifts. Some cities have contests to create the best chocolate sculpture, many of which are animal figures.

Music, Dance

Holy Week processions in Spain are filled with religious music and hymns. Spanish composer Cristóbal de Morales (c. 1500–1553) wrote many famous pieces of church music, as did Tomás Luis de Victoria (c. 1548–1611), whose music is widely performed during Holy Week and in Passion plays. Amateur actors and actresses give Passion plays throughout Spain during Holy Week in many locations, including roped-off streets, churches, and theater stages.

One of the trademarks of Easter music in Spain is the spontaneous and heartfelt *saeta,* a wailing song of grief and repentance sung by ordinary people who are deeply moved by the sight of the holy figures. These brief songs of mourning are often sung from a balcony overlooking the street. The saetas can be so striking that the processions come to a halt and the crowd grows suddenly quiet.

Bocinas and *bombos*

In many Spanish cities and villages, drums sound throughout the period of mourning for Christ's Passion and death. Nearly all the men, wearing long robes, beat drums beginning at midnight on Holy Thursday and continuing until late Saturday night, Easter Eve. In some areas, as many as ten thousand drummers participate.

The loud, steady drumbeats are called *tamboradas* (pronounced tam-boh-RAH-duhs). The brass drums used are called *bombos*. Some drummers sit in one place, while others walk up and down streets drumming for hours. Drummers wrap their hands to protect them from the steady pounding, but many men finish the ceremony with bleeding hands in spite of this precaution. In some areas, men play long horns called *bocinas* (pronounced boh-SEE-nuhs) that emit mournful sounds that recall Christ's suffering before and during the Crucifixion.

Easter eve serenades

In one old Easter custom, called the *fromajadas* (pronounced froh-muh-HAH-duhs), groups of young men go door to door on Easter eve serenading the residents with guitars or drums. They receive cheese pastries for their efforts.

Special Role of Children, Young Adults

On Palm Sunday, children carry palm branches to mass to be blessed by the priest. Boys carry undecorated branches, but the girls' branches have sweets or decorations hanging from them. Throughout Holy Week, some Spanish children take part in processions. They dress in costumes similar to those of adults and carry candles or incense.

A favorite Holy Week procession of Seville is La Borriquita (pronounced bore-ee-KEE-tuh; the Little Donkey), which is held on Palm Sunday. The main paso, or float, features Jesus' entrance into Jerusalem on a donkey. La Borriquita is presented by a boys' cofradia, some of whose members are still babies. A young people's orchestra leads the procession.

The angel descends

In some cities, including Peñafiel and Cartagena, a child dressed in an angel costume thrills the crowd in a celebration called the "Descent of the Angel." The child represents the angel who brought the news of Christ's resurrection. During a Resurrection Sunday procession in Cartagena, a child is lowered with pulleys from the clock tower in the central plaza to a statue of the Virgin Mary. In Peñafiel, the child removes Mary's veil and then releases a cage of doves.

For More Information

Goodwin, Bob, and Candi Perez. *A Taste of Spain.* New York: Thomson Learning, 1995.

Kohen, Elizabeth. *Spain.* New York: Marshall Cavendish, 1995.

Web sites

"Semana Santa." [Online] http://www.cyberspain.com/life/ssanta.htm (accessed on February 7, 2000).

Ukraine

Name of Holiday: Velykden

Introduction

Easter, called Velykden (pronounced vuh-LICK-den; Great Day), is the Ukrainian Orthodox Church's most important holiday. The celebrations combine modern innovations with ancient traditions to render the holiday one of the most enjoyable of the year. Ukraine is famous for its elaborately decorated Easter eggs.

History

Velykden, the Ukrainian word for Easter, was also the word used for the spring equinox. An equinox occurs when the length of the day's sunlight equals the length of the day's darkness. Before the arrival of Christianity, early Ukrainians acknowledged the spring equinox, which occurs around March 22, by celebrating the sun's defeat of "the unclean spirit." After Christianity, this became a celebration of Jesus' defeat of death and Satan with the Crucifixion and the Resurrection.

Easter comes to Ukraine

Christianity was first introduced in Ukraine in 954 by the ruling princess Olga

(c. 890–969), who was baptized under Greek influence and began teaching her people about her new faith. She was made the Ukrainian Orthodox Church's first saint for her efforts to spread Christianity. Her grandson Prince Vladimir I (c. 956–1015) converted his people to Christianity in 988, soon after he became a Christian. He was also made a saint.

Ukraine, then called Kievan Rus, had close political and economic ties to Greece and adopted the Eastern Orthodox Church doctrine. Easter became the most important religious holiday, as it was in the Byzantine (Eastern Roman) Empire. Eastern Roman rulers once attended Good Friday services in the Ukrainian Orthodox churches. These services became known as the Royal Hours.

An egg for the czar

Ukraine was part of the Russian Empire from the late 1600s through the early 1900s. Near the end of this period, Russian goldsmith and jeweler Peter Carl Fabergé (1846–1920) created his famous Fabergé Easter eggs for the Russian czars (rulers). The eggs are encrusted with gold and jewels and are considered priceless works of art.

Easter under Communism

For much of the time when Ukraine was part of the Union of Soviet Socialist Republics (USSR) under Communist rule (1917–91), church holidays were abolished. Many people continued to celebrate them quietly in their homes, and priests continued to hold services in secret. Hundreds of church officials were imprisoned, exiled to Siberia, or killed for their devotion.

Renewed celebrations

After Ukraine became an independent democratic nation in August 1991, the Ukrainian people began to restore old traditions and returned to celebrating Easter and other religious holidays openly and with renewed enthusiasm. The Ukrainian Orthodox Church is Ukraine's largest religious denomination, with some thirty-five million members. The Ukrainian Greek-Catholic Church is second largest, with about five million members.

Folklore, Legends, Stories

Several Ukrainian legends arose to explain the origin of the beautifully decorated Easter eggs called *pysanky* (pronounced pe-SAHN-kee; the singular is *pysanka*). One says that, as Christ suffered on the cross, wherever a drop of his blood fell a red egg appeared on the ground. As his mother, Mary, wept for him at the cross, her tears landed on the red eggs and they became decorated with elaborate designs.

A second legend says that one winter long ago, the weather turned freezing cold so suddenly that birds fell from the sky because they were too cold to fly. Peasant farmers brought the birds into their homes and kept them warm through the winter. In spring, the farmers released them, and in a few days the birds brought back a beautiful decorated egg for each peasant who had saved their lives.

It was tradition for a young woman to drop a pysanka with her name on it into a stream, hoping it would be found by her future husband. The young man who found it was likely to come calling, and a match would often be made.

Bunny nests

There are several Ukrainian folk customs and legends that involve the Easter bunny. Children would make a warm nest outside for the Easter bunny, and line the nest with grass or moss. They sometimes put materials such as onion skins in the nest as well. These natural materials would be used by the Easter bunny to make the dyes that colored her eggs. The children also planted winter wheat in a container for the bunny to eat. On Easter Sunday morning, the children would find colored eggs in their nests. When young children colored eggs at home, they were sometimes told they were helping the Easter bunny so she would have enough eggs to deliver to all the children in the world.

Ukrainian Holy Week folklore

On Holy Thursday, called Thursday of Passion, Passion candles were lit in church for reading the Bible, the holy book of Christianity. The worshipers carried their lighted candles home from church after the midnight service and, with the flame from the candles, burned the shape of a small cross into the wooden beam over their doorways. The symbol was believed to have the power to protect the household. At other times of the year, the candles might be lit during a thunderstorm, an illness, or a death.

Customs, Traditions, Ceremonies

Many Ukrainians fast during the forty days of Lent, giving up meat and animal fats. During Holy Week, they also give up eggs, dairy foods, and oils. Some priests keep a total fast for part of Holy Week. Parishioners, including older children, may fast completely for part of each day. Fasting is a way of purifying the body and mind and preparing to celebrate the Feast of the Resurrection of Christ. Some people give up music and dancing as well as foods. To further prepare for Easter, Ukrainians thoroughly clean their houses during Lent.

Palm Sunday willows

On Palm Sunday, Ukrainians gently slap one another with pussy willows in a custom called God's Wounds. People deny having tapped another person, saying it was the willow itself that did the tapping.

Creating pysanky: A spiritual art

On Holy Thursday, custom calls for the making of pysanky, the intricately decorated Easter eggs that Ukraine is famous for. They were traditionally made by the women of the house at night, after the children had been put to bed. Women prepared the day before by fasting, refraining from gossip, and holding their temper. It was believed that a woman should be in a perfect spiritual state of mind before beginning to create pysanky.

The tradition is believed to have begun several hundred years before the time of Christ (c. 6 B.C.–c. A.D. 30) and has been passed down from mother to daughter for centuries. As a woman worked on a pysanka, she was said to transfer all the family's goodness into the design so that evil would be kept away from the house. Women sang songs as they worked to soothe the spirits of dead family members thought to be present in the night. They did not socialize but worked alone, asking

An artist melting the beeswax from a nearly completed pysanka in 1995. Several legends arose to explain the origin of the beautifully decorated Ukrainian Easter eggs.
Reproduced by permission of AP/Wide World Photos.

God's blessing on each pysanka. This important tradition continues today and is practiced by Ukrainian women and those of Ukrainian descent all over the world.

Passion Friday and coloring *krashanky*

Good Friday is called Passion Friday in Ukraine. Special church services are held,

Pysanky Symbols and Colors

The many designs and symbols used to decorate Ukrainian eggs, called pysanky, have special meanings. Flowers, fruits, trees, and leaves represent the rebirth of plant life after winter. A plant in a vase represents the Tree of Life as described in the Bible, the sacred book of Christianity. Cherries represent femininity and a wish for happiness and love. A fir tree branch means youth and eternal life. Grapes represent faithful love and good will; apples or plums are believed to bring wisdom and good health. Flowers such as tulips, sunflowers, and roses are symbols of happiness and springtime. Wheat represents a wish for good health.

Animals such as horses, fish, deer, and birds are drawn in abstract. Sometimes the artist depicts only claws, teeth, or horns. Chickens are a symbol of fertility. Deer, roosters, and oak leaves are symbols of masculinity and strength, and fish symbolize prosperity as well as Christ, the "fisher of men." Butterflies represent childhood and the journey of the soul to heaven.

Geometric designs and lines fill in spaces between symbols, so the whole egg seems to be covered. "Forty triangles" is one popular design, representing the forty days of Lent or the biblical story of Christ's forty days in the desert. Ladder, sieve, and basket shapes are also popular. A double line represents a path. A never-ending line, called the "meander," is said to trap evil spirits that brush against the egg—the spirits keep following the line forever. Dots are symbolic of the tears shed by Christ's mother, Mary.

The color red on pysanky symbolizes life, joy, passion, and hope. Yellow represents fertility, a good harvest, and prosperity. Green stands for spring and new plant life. Black and white together symbolize protection from evil and honor for the dead. An older person traditionally is given pysanky with many darker colors in honor of a long, rich life. Young people receive lighter-colored pysanky with fewer designs because they have just started out in life.

and people visit the Holy Shroud (a representation of Jesus in death) at church. Many fast all day until the church service is over. Good Friday is also the day for baking Easter breads, called *paska* (pronounced POS-kuh) and *babka* (pronounced BOB-kuh).

On Holy Saturday, families color Easter eggs called *krashanky* (pronounced krah-SHAN-kee), which are boiled and dyed in plain colors. They eat them after Easter Sunday church services to break the Lenten fast and use them in Easter games. People once threw the shells of krashanky into water in honor of the dead. Children rubbed their cheeks with red krashanky to make them look rosy and healthy.

Blessing the Easter baskets

On Easter eve, the night of Holy Saturday, people take baskets filled with pysanky, krashanky, Easter breads, and other traditional Easter foods to mass to be blessed before they are eaten the next day. The basket is lined with a woven and embroidered cloth called *rushnyky* (pronounced ROOSH-neck-ee) and covered with a second rushnyky. Each family places a lighted candle on top of their loaf of paska after the mass. The priest walks up and down, blessing the baskets by sprinkling them with holy water.

Khristos Voskres!

After the Saturday night mass, the priest says joyfully, *"Khristos Voskres!"* (pronounced KREES-tos VOS-kres; "Christ is risen!"), and the people respond, *"Voistyno Voskres!"* (pronounced vo-EES-tu-noh VOS-kres; "He is risen indeed!"). Then the parishioners turn to one another and repeat the greeting and response, often giving one another three kisses on the cheek. After the Easter baskets are blessed, family members and fellow parishioners exchange pysanky from their baskets, and each family gives a pysanka to the priest for performing the blessing. Then the people take their baskets home and arrange the table for Easter dinner the next day.

On Easter Sunday, church bells ring off and on all day. People go to church Sunday morning for Easter mass. Some stop to visit the cemetery and say "Khristos Voskres!" at the graves of deceased relatives. Families once put a little mound of soil with green blades of oat sprouts growing from it on the Easter Sunday dinner table. They had started the sprouts a few weeks earlier. This "little grave" served to remind the family of relatives who had died.

Later in the day on Easter Sunday, each community holds the year's biggest religious celebration, with dancing, feasting, concerts, and arts and crafts shows. In Ukraine's capital, Kiev, many celebrations are held on Easter Sunday in Sophiesvska Square, near the nation's oldest cathedral, Saint Sophia.

Water fight!

On the Monday after Easter, in some parts of Ukraine, men and boys once splashed women and girls with water, or even poured buckets of water over their heads. On Tuesday, the girls and women had their turn and soaked the men and boys. They often used water from melted snow; this icy cold drenching was supposed to be good for the complexion and bring good luck. It also brought young people together to socialize. Today, many young Ukrainians use super water pistols to soak their friends.

The Monday and Tuesday after Easter are also important days for children to visit their grandparents and godparents. Families pack baskets of food and pysanky (Easter eggs) when they go visiting. On Tuesday, some adults dance and party as a way of bidding Easter and Holy Week farewell for another year.

Clothing, Costumes

Most Ukrainians wear Western-style clothing today, but for folk dances and festivals women and girls wear the traditional skirt and blouse with colorful embroidery. Men and boys wear embroidered vests and

A priest blesses homemade breads and pysanky on Holy Saturday in 1998. After Easter baskets are blessed, family members and fellow parishioners exchange eggs from their baskets.
Reproduced by permission of AP/Wide World Photos.

shirts and trousers. Both women and men wear boots with their outfits. Ukrainians wear their best clothes to church for the Easter Sunday service.

Foods, Recipes

Paska, Easter bread, is the most symbolic Ukrainian Easter food. It is a wheel-shaped loaf of bread, often decorated with cross-shaped dough ornaments and little dough flowers and birds. It may also have religious words or phrases written in a circle on the smooth, flat top of the loaf.

During the eighteenth and nineteenth centuries, people took wagons to church for the blessing of Easter foods instead of baskets, because the loaves of Easter bread measured perhaps two feet across. The bread was taken to church wrapped in a large scarf. Families also roasted a whole pig for the feast. Today, churches may bless such a large loaf of paska for the whole parish during the Easter Sunday service.

Foods taken to midnight mass for blessing on Holy Saturday are in small enough portions to be carried in baskets. They represent the foods that will be eaten

Paska (Ukrainian Easter Bread)

Ingredients

About 15 cups plain, sifted flour

1 cup lukewarm water

1 package (1 tablespoon) yeast

1 tablespoon honey

3 cups milk, scalded and then cooled to lukewarm

1 cup sugar

6 beaten eggs

1 stick plus 3 tablespoons melted butter

1 tablespoon salt

1 beaten egg mixed with 2 tablespoons water for glaze

Directions

1. Dissolve honey and yeast in lukewarm water and let sit for 12 minutes, then combine in a large bowl with lukewarm milk and 5 cups of the flour, stirring until smooth.

2. Cover bowl with a towel and let dough sit in a warm place for about 20 minutes or until it has begun to rise and form bubbles.

3. Stir in the 6 beaten eggs, sugar, salt, and melted butter. Then begin adding more flour, about 2 cups at a time, stirring until the dough has a medium texture, not too soft but not too stiff.

4. Turn the dough out onto a floured bread board and knead, adding more flour and kneading until the dough is dry enough so it does not stick to your hands. You should use most of the flour, and the dough should be smooth and springy.

at the Easter Sunday feast. Foods to be blessed include paska, butter, baked cheese, horseradish, beet relish, and both krashanky and pysanky (Easter eggs).

Eggs are the first food eaten to break the Lenten fast. After mass on Easter Sunday, families gather around the table. The eldest person or the head of the household divides a blessed colored egg into several parts. With the words "Christ is risen!," he or she hands each family member a portion of egg. They respond, "Truly, he is risen!" Sharing the egg sym-bolizes family unity and a wish for a prosperous year.

Foods served for Easter Sunday dinner in Ukraine today include *kovbasa* (sausage), a soup called borsch (made with beef, beets, cabbage, sour cream, and herbs), ham or roast pork, cooked vegetable salads with vinaigrette dressing, *pirozhki* (a cheese and meat pastry), *babka* (meaning "old woman"; a coffee cake), *paska* (Easter bread), horseradish, beet relish, cheesecake, and pastries. The table is decorated with pussy willows, colored eggs, and spring greenery.

5. Return dough to the bowl and cover with the towel. Let rise until it is about twice its original size. Then punch it down with your fist and let it rise again.

6. Divide the dough into three equal portions, covering one with plastic wrap and setting it aside. Form the other two portions into balls and place in greased 9-inch round springform pans. Cover with towels and let rise to the top of each pan.

7. Unwrap the third portion of dough and divide it into four equal parts.

8. Shape each quarter into a rope about 20 inches long and lay 2 ropes in a cross shape on top of each loaf.

9. Trim the ends of the horizontal rope so it looks like a cross. Use scissors or a knife to cut 6-inch-long slits into each end of the ropes and twist the cut ends together to braid them.

10. Use the snipped-off pieces of dough to make small ornaments such as flowers, birds, and leaves and place them around the cross.

11. Brush the top of the loaf and the cross with the egg-and-water mixture.

12. Bake at 400 degrees for about 15 minutes, then lower heat to 350 degrees and bake for another 25 minutes or until done. If the tops of the loaves are becoming too brown, cover them with aluminum foil toward the end of baking time.

13. To serve, remove the loaves from the pans and let them cool.

Makes 2 loaves

Arts, Crafts, Games

Ukrainians make two kinds of Easter eggs: krashanky, which are boiled eggs decorated with simple colors and designs, and pysanky, which are given as gifts and treasured for years. Pysanky are often considered works of art and are handed down from one generation to another. The art of decorating pysanky is called *pysanka,* meaning "written egg," from the Ukrainian verb *pysaty,* which means "to write." The eggs symbolize renewal at Easter through Christ's resurrection.

Pysanky were traditionally made for other religious and social occasions as well as for Easter. They are given away as gifts of friendship, love, and respect. Pysanky can be made from chicken, goose, quail, or even ostrich eggs.

Making pysanky

Most pysanky are made using the wax-resist, or batik (pronounced ba-TEEK), method. Before or after the egg is decorated, the egg yolk and white are blown out of the shell. This is done by making a small hole in the top and the bottom of the eggshell and blowing on one end so that the contents slowly run out.

A special writing instrument called the *kistka* (pronounced KIST-kuh) is used to apply wax to designs drawn lightly in pencil on the egg. A funnel attached to the kistka is filled with wax, which is kept flowing by passing the tip of the kistka through a flame every few minutes.

Pysanky are dipped in dyes of different colors, beginning with the lightest colors first and proceeding to black. With each dipping, the areas covered with wax remain the color of the egg before the dipping, because the dye cannot color through the wax. The colors used most are red, yellow or orange, green, blue, white, and black. Ukrainians once used natural plant dyes such as roots, tree bark, plant leaves, and animal skins to make the dyes. Most dyes used today are made from chemicals. With each dipping, wax is used to shield areas of the egg that are not to be colored at that time.

When the pysanka is complete, the entire egg is covered with hardened wax. The wax is removed by holding the egg near a flame and then wiping off the melted wax. The wax can be removed faster by putting all the pysanky into an oven (after the contents have been drained) just hot enough to melt the wax and then wiping off the eggs. When complete, pysanky are painted with shellac to preserve them. It takes about eight hours to make a pysanka—about six of those to draw the designs. Older pysanky are considered works of art and are often displayed in museums.

Ukrainian religious icons

Like Greece, Ukraine is famous for its religious paintings on wood panels, called icons. People worshiped and prayed to the icons and believed they had the power to work miracles. Many Ukrainian artists painted these icons as a way to seek forgiveness for their sins. The various paintings, completed from the tenth through the sixteenth centuries, were housed in churches, where people could see them regularly. Today, most of the paintings are exhibited in museums. Many artists did not sign their paintings because they believed the inspiration for them was owed to God. Legends tell of painters who received guidance from angels.

Embroidered cloths

Ukrainian women are famous for the beautiful, multicolored embroidery they do on the woven cloths called rushnyky, which are used to line and cover Easter baskets to be blessed in church on Holy Saturday. Rushnyky are also hung over religious icons to protect them.

Easter egg rolls

A popular Ukrainian Easter game is for children to use colored eggs like marbles. They roll the eggs around on the grass, trying to tap other players' eggs and crack them. Winners get to keep any egg they crack. In another Easter game, each player rolls an egg down a tilted board, aiming for another player's egg at the bottom. If a player's egg hits another egg, the player gets to keep both eggs.

Music, Dance

On Easter Sunday, in church courtyards and in the streets, Ukrainians celebrate by feasting and dancing *hahilki* (pronounced hah-HEEL-kee), traditional circle dances done to Ukrainian folk music. Today, hahilki is most often performed by girls who belong to youth organizations.

Traditional Ukrainian musical instruments are the *bandura* (pronounced ban-DOOR-ruh), a string instrument resembling a lute; the *sopilka* (pronounced so-PEEL-kuh), a type of flute; the *trembita* (pronounced trem-BEE-tuh), a hollow wooden tube wrapped with birch bark; and the *tsymbaly* (pronounced tsim-BAH-lee), a string instrument similar to a hammered dulcimer.

The Ukrainian composer Nikolai Diletsky (c. 1630–c. 1680) wrote classical Easter hymns that are still sung by choirs today in many parts of the world. He composed the music for a famous Easter piece, the *Kanon of the Resurrection,* written by Saint John of Damascus, who died in 749. The *Russian Easter Festival Overture,* written by Russian composer Nikolay A. Rimsky-Korsakov (1844–1908), is also a popular classical piece for Easter in Ukraine. An important part of Ukraine's Easter music is the chanting by priests in the churches.

Special Role of Children, Young Adults

Ukrainian children participate in Lenten fasting, help color eggs, play egg games, do folk dances, and attend church services with their families during the Easter season. Young children may make bunny nests and wait for the Easter bunny to bring colored eggs. Girls learn how to make pysanky from their mothers, a craft they will develop year after year as they grow up and will pass along to their own daughters.

On Easter Monday and Tuesday, children and young adults soak one another with water pistols, carrying on the old water-splashing tradition. Grandparents and godparents love getting an Easter visit from the children. In some areas, visiting continues through the entire week after Easter Sunday.

For More Information

Bassis, Vladimir. *Ukraine.* Milwaukee: Gareth Stevens, 1998.

Clay, Rebecca. *Ukraine: A New Independence.* New York: Benchmark Books, 1997.

Web sites

"How to Make Ukrainian Easter Eggs." [Online] http://www3.ns.sympatico.ca/amorash/ukregg .html (accessed on February 7, 2000).

"The Symbolism of the Ukrainian Easter Egg." (Adapted from a story by Sofia Zielyk.) [Online] http://www.uazone.net/holidays/ EasterEggs.html (accessed on February 7, 2000).

Easter Sources

DuBois, Jill. *Colombia.* New York: Marshall Cavendish, 1991, pp. 51, 71 80–81, 87–89, 111.

Griffin, Robert H., and Ann H. Shurgin, eds. *The Folklore of World Holidays.* 2nd ed. Farmington Hills, Mich.: Gale, 1999, pp. 227, 232, 238–40.

McKay, Susan. *Spain.* Milwaukee: Gareth Stevens, 1999, pp. 12–15.

Thompson, Sue Ellen, ed. *Holiday Symbols 1998.* Detroit, Mich.: Omnigraphics, 1998, pp. 106–12.

Tracz, Orysia Paszczak. "Ukrainian Easter Traditions: Velykden—Great Day." *Ukrainian Weekly,* April 23, 1995. [Online, Electric Library]

Wagstaff, Kathy. "Traditions Mark Holiest Season: Celebrations of Passover and Easter." *Atlanta Journal and Constitution,* March 25, 1999, pp. JQ01. [Online, Electric Library]

Webb, Lois Sinaiko. *Holidays of the World Cookbook for Students*. Phoenix, Ariz.: Oryx Press, 1995, pp. 100, 235–36.

Web sites

"The Black Madonna." [Online] http://www.theworkofgod.org/Aparitns/Others2.htm (accessed on February 24, 2000).

"The Blessing of the Easter Basket." [Online] http://www.ukemonde.com/easter/blessing.htm (accessed on February 24, 2000).

"Easter." [Online] http://www.clark.net/pub/jumpsam/fiestas/easter.htm (accessed on February 24, 2000).

"Easter Customs." [Online] http://www.puffin.ptialaska.net/~klayj/custom.htm (accessed on February 24, 2000).

"Easter: Its Origins and Meanings." [Online] wysiwyg://1/http://www.religioustolerance.org/easter.htm (accessed on February 24, 2000).

"Easter in Poland." [Online] http://www.polstore.com/html/polisheaster.html (accessed on February 24, 2000).

"Facts About Greece." [Online] http://www.greek-embassy.org/press/facts/index.html (accessed on February 24, 2000).

"Holy Week." [Online] http://www.mompox.click2site.com/english/holy_week.htm (accessed on February 24, 2000).

"Poland." [Online] http://www.expedia.msn.co.uk/daily/places/Easter (accessed on February 24, 2000).

Ranger, Aiesha M. "Pysanky." [Online] http://www.weblodge.com/current/pysanky (accessed on February 24, 2000).

Teague, Lettie. "Easter in Athens." [Online] http://pathfinder.com/FoodWine/804/easter.html (accessed on February 24, 2000).

Ukrainian Museum, New York. "Pysanky—Easter Eggs." [Online] http://www.brama.com/ukrainian_museum/pysanky.html (accessed on February 24, 2000).

Halloween and Festivals of the Dead

Also Known As:
Ching Ming Festival (China)
Obon Festival (Japan)
El Día de los Muertosor Day of the Dead (Mexico)
Halloween (United Kingdom, United States)

Introduction

Festivals in honor of the dead are celebrated in countries throughout the world and are called by various names. In the United States and many other countries, the festival is called Halloween and is quite a popular holiday. Occurring at the end of October, Halloween was originally a harvest festival, a time for gathering the last of the crops from the fields and returning cattle to the barns in preparation for winter. Over time, it has developed into a boisterous celebration that includes parties, Halloween parades, and dressing in costume to go door to door for treats.

The Chinese Ching Ming Festival is a spring festival honoring the dead. During this festival, people thoroughly clean their houses and family shrines. The shrines include statues of Buddha and special items that remind the family of relatives who have died. To celebrate Ching Ming, people in China also visit cemeteries and participate in candlelight vigils, fairs, and parades.

The ancient Japanese festival known as Obon is celebrated in honor of deceased family members and ancestors, much like El Día de los Muertos, or Day of the Dead, in Mexico. Mexico's Day of the Dead, celebrated at the beginning of November, is one of the most popular holidays in Mexico. People visit and clean graves and prepare food for the dead. Children parade through the streets shouting "Calaveras!" ("Skulls!") and are given money and candy, similar to trick-or-treating in other countries.

History

Some scholars believe that Halloween began with the Celtic (pronounced KEL-tick) peoples who lived in Ireland, Scotland, England, Wales, and northern France before the birth of Jesus Christ, more than two thousand years ago. They held an annual festival called Samhain (pronounced SOW-en) that marked the end of the fall harvest and the beginning of winter. It was a time for harvesting the last of the grains, fruits, and vegetables and for herding cattle down from hilly summer pastures. Some animals were slaughtered to provide families with food for the long, cold winter.

Holiday Fact Box: Halloween and Festivals of the Dead

Themes

Halloween celebrates the supernatural and the spooky; people dress up in costumes, go trick-or-treating, play practical jokes, and make mischief. Festivals of the dead honor the spirits of dead family members and ancestors and are celebrated by visiting cemeteries, cleaning graves and tombs, feasting, and watching parades.

Type of Holiday

Halloween and festivals of the dead are largely nonreligious folk holidays. They are not considered national holidays in any country, but they are quite popular and widely celebrated.

When Celebrated

Halloween is celebrated on October 31. The Ching Ming Festival is held in April; the Obon Festival is held in July or August; and Day of the Dead celebrations are held on October 31, November 1 (All Saints' Day), and November 2 (All Souls' Day).

Samhain: The eve of wandering spirits

Because the Celts were farmers and herdsmen, the end of harvest marked the end of their year, and so Samhain was also regarded as the beginning of the Celtic New Year. To the Celts, turning points in nature, such as the point where land meets sky, sea meets shore, day meets night, and season meets season, were times when unusual things might happen. Because Samhain represented the turning of summer into winter and the old year into the new, it was considered the strangest time of year—a time when the boundary between the world of the dead and the world of the living became very thin and the spirits of the dead could return to earth.

To commemorate the return of spirits from the world of the dead—or perhaps to ward off witches and other unwelcome forces—Celtic priests, called Druids, lit sacred bonfires on this night. People burned crops and animals in the bonfires as sacrifices to the Celtic gods. It is also thought that on Samhain the Celts dressed in costumes made of animal heads and skins, either to imitate the spirits of the dead or to keep from being recognized by wandering spirits that might try to possess their bodies.

Because Samhain was such a powerful time for spirits, the Celts believed the future could be foretold on this evening, and they engaged in many forms of divination, or fortune-telling. Celtic legends also tell of heroic deeds accomplished by great warriors on the eve of Samhain.

A brew of Celtic and Christian beliefs

As Christianity arrived in the British Isles about fifteen hundred years ago, Church leaders tried to stop the Celts' pagan religious practices and festival customs, but the people held on to their traditions. In about A.D. 834, Pope Gregory IV declared November 1 All Saints' Day to honor the saints and martyrs who had no special feast days of their own. The holiday was also called Hallowmas (All Saints' Mass), and the night before Hallowmas came to be known as All Hallows' Eve. During the Middle Ages (c. A.D. 500 to 1500), All Hallows' Eve became known as a powerful time for witches and sorcerers.

In about A.D. 1000, the Church made November 2 All Souls' Day, a day for honoring the faithful Christian dead. These Church celebrations to honor the spirits of the dead and the souls of the saints fit in well with the traditional Celtic practices.

Halloween comes to North America

Irish and Scottish immigrants first introduced Halloween customs to the United States during the 1700s. Settlers in the southern colonies were especially drawn to the divination, or fortune-telling, practices of All Hallows' Eve. English settlers of the New England colonies were more inclined to celebrate the church holiday All Saints' Day rather than tell ghost stories and try to predict the future.

During the middle 1800s, thousands of Irish and Scots immigrated to the United States and Canada. The Irish introduced more divination games, the lighting of jack-o'-lanterns, the popular game bobbing for apples, and the playing of Halloween pranks. Scottish immigrants introduced the Halloween custom of "guising" (pronounced GUY-zing), or dressing in costume and collecting treats. The Scots also introduced Americans to the poetry of Robert Burns (1750–1796), their national poet, who described Scottish Halloween games in his poem "Halloween."

During the late 1800s, these Irish and Scottish customs blended with North American fall harvest celebrations. Halloween became a time for parties, often given by young ladies and featuring food, music and dancing, games like bobbing for apples, and divination games to predict a future sweetheart or spouse. In the countryside, young men played boisterous pranks at Halloween just as their fathers had done in Ireland.

Halloween trick-or-treating became increasingly popular and widespread in the United States and Canada between the 1920s and the 1950s, and Halloween became primarily a children's holiday. Children at first dressed in simple, homemade costumes, but store-bought costumes imitating popular television, movie, and storybook characters became available by the mid-1900s.

Since that time, trick-or-treating has continued in the United States and Canada, and Halloween has grown into a popular celebration that also features parades, costume contests with extravagant prizes, and "haunted" houses that draw crowds of thrill seekers.

Festivals of the dead in Asia

Holidays for honoring the dead are celebrated throughout Asia. The Ching Ming Festival in China probably began as early as 200 B.C. It was at first a time to enjoy the beginning of spring with outdoor activities such as kite flying, picnics, festivals, and hunts. The festival gradually became associated with honoring the dead, an ancient Chinese practice that was further encouraged by the revered Chinese philosopher Confucius (551–479 B.C.). Ching Ming grew into a festival that includes visiting

Girls dressed as witches trick-or-treat on rollerblades in Makati, the Philippines, on Halloween 1996. The practice of begging for sweets at Halloween may have roots in the Middle Ages when the poor begged for "sweet soul cakes" on All Souls' Day. Reproduced by permission of AP/Wide World Photos.

graves, planting trees in cemeteries, and making offerings to the spirits of the dead.

Japan's Obon Festival, a Buddhist holiday for honoring the dead, has been celebrated since seventh-century Buddhist priests began offering a share of their food to the ancestors at this time of year. At first, only the Japanese noblemen joined the priests in their celebration, but as the years passed, all Buddhist families joined in honoring their ancestors. Today, the Obon Festival is a major holiday throughout Japan.

The Day of the Dead in Mexico

In Mexico, festivals to honor the dead have been celebrated for hundreds of years, beginning in the fifteenth century when the Aztec Indians controlled the region. These early festivals honored the Aztec god of death, and were held during harvest time. When the Spanish began to explore Mexico in the 1500s, they introduced the Roman Catholic religion and brought with them the traditions and customs of Christianity. The rituals connected with All Saints' Day and All Souls' Day combined with the native festivals to eventually become the important holiday El Día de los Muertos, the Day of the Dead.

Folklore, Legends, Stories

Many Western Halloween folktales, as well as classic stories and poems, are about ghosts, witches, goblins, elves, or fairies. American poet and short-story writer Edgar Allan Poe (1809–1849) and American author Washington Irving (1783–1859) wrote on these themes, as did Scottish poet Robert Burns (1750–1796) and English poet and dramatist William Shakespeare (1564–1616). Thousands of others have written ghost stories, both modern and classic, and ghost tales have been told by ordinary folk since storytelling began.

Asian stories and beliefs about the dead

In most Asian countries, people believe that the spirits of the dead are still with the living and must be honored so they will remain peaceful and helpful instead of becoming angry and destructive. Chinese folklore is filled with legends about spirits of the dead who did not receive proper burial and come back to earth to seek revenge upon the living. There are also many folktales that explain some of the customs of Ching Ming. A well-known tale is about Chu, the loyal Chinese administrator who was smothered by fire in a cave in ancient China. In honor of Chu, no hot food is eaten on Cold Food Day.

The Japanese believe that the souls of the dead return to the land of the living during the Obon Festival, and that those souls combine to form one entity called *O Shorai Sama*, who is said to come riding a white horse on the first evening of the festi-

"Halloween Visitor"

The moon across the velvet sky was creep-
ing, creeping;
The very shadows seemed to lie sleeping,
sleeping;
When suddenly beside the shed,
A ghostly shape without a head
Sprang up and like a phantom fled, leap-
ing, leaping.

I followed where the autumn leaves were
sighing, sighing;
I saw the pumpkins in the sheaves, lying,
lying;
The phantom ran without a sound,
Then swifter than a hunting hound
It vanished at a single bound, flying, flying.

—*Frances Ford and Nadine Bensley*

Source: Lilla Belle Pitts, Mabelle Glenn, Lorrain E.
Watters, and Louis G. Wersen, eds. Singing
Together. Boston: Ginn and Company, 1960, p.
107.

val. Japanese and other Asian Buddhists believe that each family's ancestors continue to love living family members, and that the living should pray for and make offerings to the dead to prevent their souls from suffering.

A look at the lighter side of death in Mexico

Much Latin American folklore and literature is based on the idea that the spirits of the dead still act in the world of the living, especially during the Day of the Dead. Some of these beliefs probably originated with the Aztec and other Indians who were native to Mexico before Spanish colonization began in the 1500s. Others were introduced by Spanish authors and playwrights like José Zorrilla y Moral (1817–1893), who immigrated to Mexico as head of the national theater during the mid-1800s. At the end of his play *Don Juan Tenorio,* the main character wrestles with spirits in a cemetery. The play is still one of the most popular in Mexico, and is performed throughout Day of the Dead festivities.

Customs, Traditions, Ceremonies

In the West, the activity most associated with Halloween is trick-or-treating. The practice of begging for sweets at Halloween may have roots in the Middle Ages when the poor begged for "sweet soul cakes" on All Souls' Day. In exchange for the cakes, they promised to say prayers for the souls of the dead. The Church encouraged the handing out of soul cakes to counter the ancient Celtic practice of leaving food and drink for roaming spirits. This practice was called "going a-souling." Over time, children began to go from house to house and were given food, ale, and money.

Dressing in costume on Halloween also began in the Middle Ages. On Halloween, when ghosts were thought to roam the earth, people sometimes wore masks if they left home after dark so the ghosts would think they were spirits and let them pass unharmed.

Halloween trick-or-treating began in the United States in the middle 1800s with the arrival of many people from Ireland, who came because of food shortages in their country. They brought their Halloween customs with them, and by the early twentieth century American children were dressing in costumes and going door to door asking for sweets or money.

Over the years, trick-or-treating gained in popularity, and by the 1950s, most children in the United States participated. The practice spread to Canada, the United Kingdom (where Halloween had been losing popularity), and recently to Mexico, Japan, France, Germany, and other countries.

Today on Halloween, children dress in costumes and go from door to door shouting "trick or treat!" and are given candy or other treats. "Trick or treat!" is meant as a mild threat, meaning a trick might be played on those who do not give treats. Few children play pranks on their neighbors, however, and the majority of adults look forward to handing out candy to children on Halloween.

Other Halloween activities

Many teens and adults in the West love Halloween as much as children do. They attend costume parties, hold parades, or decorate their homes with spider webs, eerie lighting, and figures of ghosts, witches, or bats swinging from trees to thrill children who come knocking on Halloween night. The jack-o'-lantern, a pumpkin carved with a scary face and lit with a candle placed inside, is an enduring holiday symbol that sits on nearly every porch at Halloween. Communities often design a "haunted" house for an extra scare on this night of spirits. Hayrides are also popular for Halloween get-togethers.

An evil-looking jack-o'-lantern and a corpse greet visitors to a "haunted" house in Norcross, Georgia, in 1999. Communities often design a haunted house for an extra scare on Halloween. Reproduced by permission of AP/Wide World Photos.

Asian celebrations to honor the dead

During Asian festivals of the dead, people visit cemeteries and clean and decorate the graves of family ancestors. Special items and foods are placed on home or cemetery altars so that they may be enjoyed by the dead, and many families welcome the spirits of deceased relatives to the dinner table.

People burn paper clothes, cars, houses, and money as offerings to the dead, believing their essence reaches the spirits through smoke. A separate Asian festival of the dead is held in summer. Called the Hungry Ghosts Festival, it is a time when people burn these items as offerings to the spirits of those who died by violence or far from their families. The living care for these spirits so they will go calmly back to the land of the dead and not harm the living.

Japanese families leave lights and lanterns burning on the eve of the Obon Festival so that the spirits of the dead can find their way. On the final day of the festival, many Japanese participate in a ceremony in which paper lanterns fastened to a small straw boat are set out on a river to guide the spirits back to the land of the dead.

Mexico's Day of the Dead customs

During Mexico's Day of the Dead, families welcome the spirits of relatives who have died by preparing special altars in their homes. They decorate them with flowers, candles, incense, photographs, and items the relatives liked while they were alive. They also clean, weed, and decorate graves and repaint crypts in pastel colors. They prepare many foods, including those favored by the dead, and bake or buy breads and pastries in the shape of skulls and skeletons.

Family members visit cemeteries for an all-night candlelight vigil on November 1, when the spirits of deceased adults are said to return home. Cemeteries become beautiful scenes of celebration as hundreds come with candles, flowers, and baskets of food. On October 31, Mexican people visit homes where children have died. They bring toys and candy for the spirits of the dead children.

Other Day of the Dead celebrations include street plays and performances, dances, and feasting. Halloween trick-or-treating customs have also reached Mexico and other parts of Latin America from the United States. Many children put on Halloween costumes and go out to get treats during the Day of the Dead. Young people often go to Halloween parties and dances. Because they are afraid that the Mexican traditions will be overshadowed, and perhaps forgotten, many adults do not like it that these customs have become part of the Day of the Dead.

Clothing, Costumes

When it comes to Halloween costumes, almost anything goes. Children dress in traditional witch and ghost costumes, but they also create elaborate outfits to look like foods, such as slices of pizza and jars of jelly beans, unpopular politicians, or characters in the year's biggest movie hits. Whatever people can imagine is what they can become, provided they can either create it or find it in a costume shop. Materials for a Halloween costume can range from items as simple as a cardboard box, construction paper, pipe cleaners, and old clothes to designer costumes and Hollywood movie makeup.

Many adults like to dress up as much as children do on Halloween. Costumes are becoming more sophisticated, more authentic looking, and much more of a commercial success for shops that sell or rent elaborate Halloween disguises. Such disguises may help wearers win cash prizes in costume contests.

Even pets have begun to celebrate Halloween. Stores are beginning to stock a whole new category of costumes just for them. Some popular pet disguises include fairy costumes for cats and cat costumes for dogs.

People who celebrate the Ching Ming and Obon festivals do not dress in costumes, but special clothes do feature in some of the festivities. Many people in China and other Asian countries make or buy paper clothes for the dead, which are sometimes wrapped neatly in parcels, addressed to deceased family members, and then burned in offering to the spirits. In Japan, everyone wears new clothes for the Obon Festival. A special summer kimono is worn for the traditional folk dance, the Bon-Odori, held during the festival.

Western-style Halloween costumes are becoming more and more popular for children to wear during Mexico's Day of the Dead, even though some parents protest. Traditional costumes are worn by "mummers," people in disguise who parade through town each night of the festival, performing skits and playing music. The mummers wear masks that resemble characters from Mexican folklore. Another very popular Day of the Dead costume is the skeleton, which consists of white bones drawn against a black background. Contests are held to reward the person with the best skeleton costume.

Foods, Recipes

In Western countries, foods that are harvested in the fall are popular at Halloween, especially apples, pumpkins, and corn. Apples are baked, coated with caramel or candy coating, or served as hot apple cider. Many desserts are made from pumpkin, the most recognized symbol of the harvest, including pumpkin pie, pumpkin bread, and pumpkin cookies. Corn is popped and is enjoyed on chilly fall evenings. Popcorn balls are a favorite treat for Halloween parties and are sometimes given to trick-or-treaters.

Asian families prepare special foods for the spirits of the dead during the Ching Ming Festival and the Obon Festival. In China, some families still observe the Cold Food Feast on the day before Ching Ming, a day when household fires were once forbidden. This custom calls for placing uncooked rice and noodles and raw,

A boy dressed as a sonic hedgehog plays with a kitten dressed as an angel in Middlefield, Ohio, in 1999. Even pets have begun to celebrate Halloween. Reproduced by permission of AP/Wide World Photos.

unpeeled fruit and vegetables on graves as offerings to the dead.

Japanese families prepare favorite foods for their deceased loved ones and set plates for them at the table. Only vegetarian foods are placed near the family's altar for the dead on the first night of Obon, because tradition forbids the taking of life on this day. Special rice dumplings are prepared on the final day of the Obon Festival to help send the spirits on their way back to the land of the dead.

During the Day of the Dead in Mexico, families prepare their deceased loved ones' favorite foods so that the visiting spirits can enjoy the essence, or aroma, of the foods. On November 3, after the spirits have returned to the land of the dead, the living enjoy the food, since the dead have already taken their share. The Day of the Dead is also an important time of year for bakeries, which fill their shop windows with ghoulish-looking pastries in the shape of skulls, skeletons, and coffins.

Arts, Crafts, Games

Halloween decorations and art in Western countries usually feature fantasy characters on a supernatural theme. Familiar subjects include a witch riding a broom with a black cat nearby, bats, grinning jack-o'-lanterns, ghosts and goblins, fairies and elves, skeletons, and vampires with bloody fangs. Many of these characters came from Ireland, Scotland, and Wales, where folk beliefs in fairies, witches, and goblins date back hundreds of years. Fall harvest symbols such as pumpkins, corn shocks, and scarecrows are also featured in Halloween arts and crafts.

Glowing pumpkins by the door

One of the most popular activities for Halloween is carving a jack-o'-lantern, a custom that came from the British Isles, where children once carved lanterns from large turnips, gourds, and beets. Jack-o'-lanterns are made from pumpkins of any size. After a small circle is cut from the top and the seeds are scooped out, a frightening face or a design such as a haunted house or ghost is carved through the rind and flesh of the pumpkin. Then a candle is placed inside to make the design glow. Jack-o'-lanterns are usually set on porches or in windows on Halloween night.

Paper luxuries, kites, and vegetable carvings

In China and other Asian countries, making paper models of fine cars, mansions, sedan chairs fit for a king, jewelry, and expensive clothing has become an art. These items are intricately designed in rich colors for those who want their ancestors to have the very best in death, even if they were poor in life. Some of the models are five or six feet high and are created in great detail, even though they will soon be burned so that the dead may enjoy them in the afterworld.

Kite making is another popular craft in China, and the Ching Ming Festival is one of the favorite times of the year for flying kites. The kites are often hand painted with beautiful scenes from Chinese legends. Some are also designed to perform stunts or to emit special sounds in the wind.

Japanese Buddhists enjoy carving vegetables into animal shapes to decorate their home altars for the Obon Festival. Many of these are adorned with noodles, grasses, leaves, and stems to add extra detail.

Skeletons, *arcos,* and banners

During the Day of the Dead, one of the most familiar sights in Mexico is the *calacas* (pronounced kah-LOCK-uhs), funny little skeleton figurines dressed as cab drivers and schoolteachers, farmers and doctors, entertainers and secretaries. Every type of occupation is represented, perhaps to show that death comes to everyone, no matter what their profession. Children also love the little skeleton toys with movable parts that bounce up and down on springs.

Among other Mexican arts and crafts for the Day of the Dead are the lovely *arcos,* made by the men and boys of Janitzio Island in northwestern Mexico. These frames made from sticks are covered with every imaginable Day of the Dead decoration—flowers, fruits, sugar skulls, animal figures, and calacas.

In other cities and towns, artisans create tissue banners using finely cut designs of birds, angels, crosses and skeletons. These are displayed in color for the *angelitos* (spirits of children who have died), and in black and white for the spirits of adults.

Party games and contests

Some favorite traditional Western Halloween games and party pastimes are bobbing for apples and telling ghost stories. Many jack-o'-lantern carving contests are also held.

To play bobbing for apples, players kneel around a tub of water that has several apples floating on top. They try to see who can be the first to grab an apple, using only their teeth. This often involves forcing an apple to the bottom of the tub of water in order to grab it. Today in Scotland, younger children play "forking for apples," in which each player stands on a chair over the tub of apples with a fork held in his mouth, pointing downward. When the players release their forks, they hope to skewer an apple.

In China, kite-flying contests and exhibits are often held during the Ching Ming Festival, after the tombs have been cleaned and offerings have been made to

Symbols associated with Halloween tend to be supernatural in nature. Most of these symbols, including witches, black cats, and bats, can be traced to folk beliefs of Ireland, Scotland, and Wales. Reproduced by permission of AP/Wide World Photos.

the ancestors. Most kites are handmade and range from the simplest diamond-shaped paper kites to elaborate stunt kites.

In Mexico, children enjoy the large family and community gatherings during the Day of the Dead and often play together outside the cemetery gates while adults keep a graveside vigil. Children also love to dress in costume and follow bands of mummers from street to street, making up stories about spirits of the dead and collecting money and treats.

Symbols

Festivals that honor the dead include symbols that may seem somewhat ghoulish. During El Día de los Muertos in Mexico, shop windows are filled with bread formed into skeleton shapes. A typical sweet is the sugar skull. The skeleton and the skull are both symbols of the dead, but in Mexico they are presented in a light-hearted, even whimsical way. By embracing death with fun and humor, instead of fear and horror, the people of Mexico show a different attitude toward death and the dead.

In Mexico and in Asian countries, the dead are honored and welcomed during certain times of the year, when their spirits are believed to actually return to walk among the living. In Japan, families speak to the dead at the dinner table and in the home as if they were still alive. In China and other Asian countries, the dead are believed to continue to need food, houses, money, and clothing, which they can receive through smoke when paper models of these items are burned. Asian peoples have honored their ancestors for thousands of years, and they believe that the spirits of those who have died continue to watch over and care for the living, just as the living continue to care for the dead during the Ching Ming and Obon Festivals.

Because Halloween has its roots in ancient Celtic festivals that involved ghosts and spirits, symbols associated with Halloween in the West also tend to be supernatural in nature. Most of these symbols, including witches, black cats, and bats, can be traced to these early beginnings. Because Halloween was also considered a harvest festival, other symbols associated with Halloween are pumpkins, scarecrows, and corn shocks.

The witch

The witch is one of the most popular Halloween symbols. She is often portrayed as an ugly, old woman wearing a black robe and pointed black hat. She may be riding a broomstick or stirring a cauldron of witch's brew, and is usually accompanied by her faithful assistant, a black cat.

The term "witch" comes from the Saxon *witega,* meaning a wise person, prophet, or sorcerer. Witches were later associated with mischievous fairies in the folklore of Scotland and Ireland. They were blamed for all sorts of unexplained occurrences, from things as simple as spoiling milk to such deeds as stealing babies and children.

The Church believed that witches worshiped Satan and cast spells to help him do evil deeds. These beliefs became common in about the ninth and tenth centuries, and by the end of the Middle Ages, about 1500, the Church began condemning people to death for practicing witchcraft. During the sixteenth and seventeenth centuries, thousands of people were executed as witches in Europe.

The fear of witchcraft took hold in the American colonies as well, and some fifty people were hung as witches in New England. Most of the hangings took place near the town of Salem, Massachusetts, following witchcraft trials held in 1692.

Halloween was said to be the most important day of the year for witches. Halloween marked the occasion of a great witches' sabbat (midnight gathering), when covens (organized groups of witches) met to perform special rituals and welcome new members to the clan. Witches, like spirits of the dead, were believed to roam about on Halloween night, seeking to harm whomever crossed their path.

The misunderstood bat

Artificial bats are one of the most popular Halloween decorations. They are usually hung from trees or in doorways, where they swoop in the wind and can tap unsuspecting trick-or-treaters on the head. The bat is connected to Halloween for several reasons. One reason is that people believe bats are bloodthirsty. In reality, only three of the world's nearly one thousand species of bats, the vampire bats of Central and South America, feed on fresh blood. These bats bite animals with their sharp teeth and drink their blood, like Count Dracula and other vampires of horror films and novels.

Because most bats live in caves, where they sleep during the day and hibernate all winter, they are further associated with fictional vampires, who cannot bear the light of day. Also, bats have large wings that fold over their bodies with an eerie similarity to Count Dracula's long black cloak.

"Wool of bat" is one of the ingredients used by the three witches to make their brew in the play *Macbeth*, written by English playwright William Shakespeare (1564–1616). According to superstition, witches are said to rub bats' blood on their skin before casting a spell.

Shape-shifters and tempest raisers

Superstition and fear have surrounded the cat—particularly the black cat—for probably two thousand years. A god in the form of a cat was worshiped in ancient Egypt, and many royal families kept cats as honored pets. But in early Greece and Rome, people thought witches could

A girl dressed as a witch watches over a pumpkin patch near the Eiffel Tower in Paris, France, in 1997. During the Middle Ages people believed that witches, like spirits of the dead, roamed about on Halloween night. Reproduced by permission of AP/Wide World Photos.

transform women into cats and keep them as helpers, or "familiars," in working their magic. In Celtic Europe, cats were often thrown into bonfires on Samhain because they were thought to be witches in disguise.

In early Ireland, superstitions about cats were always connected with evil and witches. In the 1500s and 1600s, sailors feared storms at sea, which people thought witches created by using black cats to cast spells. Today, some people still believe it is bad luck if a black cat crosses their path.

Bats: More Good than Harm

Many people fear bats because they don't really understand the mysterious night animals. Some people believe bats can get tangled in a person's hair, others think that all bats suck the blood of humans and animals, and many consider them a threat because bats can carry rabies. Bats are actually one of the most beneficial creatures of nature. They eat billions of crop-damaging insects, mosquitoes, and other pests each year.

Today, just over half of the United States' forty-four species of bats are in danger of losing their homes as caves and abandoned mines are closed off. Some people who fear bats burn them, and large bat colonies are sometimes killed by groups of vandals. If bats are disturbed from their hibernation in winter, the young may die. In 1982, an organization called Bat Conservation International (BCI) was founded to help educate people about the benefits of bats and to help them survive.

The jack-o'-lantern

A pumpkin carved with spooky eyes, a triangle nose, and big crooked teeth that has a candle flickering inside it is called a jack-o'-lantern, and it is one of the most well-known Halloween symbols. Jack-o'-lanterns were first made in Great Britain and Ireland, where they were carved from large turnips, gourds, and beets.

When Scotch-Irish immigrants landed in America, they found the native pumpkin made a better jack-o'-lantern than the vegetables they had carved in Great Britain. By the turn of the twentieth century, children in some parts of the United States had begun to dress in costumes on Halloween and carry jack-o'-lanterns from house to house, holding the grinning, candlelit faces to greet anyone opening the door.

The jack-o'-lantern has remained the foremost Halloween symbol, and today some pumpkin carvers compete for prizes with their elaborate jack-o'-lantern designs made with special pumpkin-carving patterns and tools. As a Halloween decoration, jack-o'-lanterns of different sizes are sometimes stacked to make "totem poles." Some children even dress in jack-o'-lantern costumes on Halloween.

Music, Dance

In Western countries, Halloween has been considered a children's holiday since the early 1900s, and dozens of children's Halloween songs have been written. Many are about witches and goblins, while others are about autumn and the harvest. Music is a popular part of the the Day of the Dead in Mexico, where mummers in costume play and sing as they stroll through town and present humorous skits.

In Japan, a highlight of the Obon Festival is the Japanese folk dance festival called the Bon-Odori, or "Dance of Rejoicing." These festivals are lit by lanterns, and are held throughout Japan in public parks and town squares. The dances are also held in Buddhist temples. Some of the Japanese dances resemble Western-style folk dances, but others are very traditional Japanese, featuring graceful and intricate movements and postures and a lot of spinning and hand clapping. The dancers are accompanied by music played mainly on drums and flutes.

China

Name of Holiday: Ching Ming Festival

Introduction

Ching Ming, or Qing Ming, is a spring festival held on April 5 or 6, exactly 106 days after the winter solstice (around December 21) and two weeks after the spring equinox (around March 21). Both the solstice and the equinox have to do with cycles of the sun.

At the winter solstice, the sun is at the lowest point in the sky; at the summer solstice, the sun has risen to the highest point in the sky. An equinox occurs when the length of the day's sunlight is equal to the length of the day's darkness. This happens only twice a year—once in the spring and once in the fall. Many ancient festivals were celebrated during these times because they correspond to turning points in nature and were thought to be magical.

The name Ching Ming means "pure and bright" or "clear and bright," and refers to the clear, bright spring days on which the festival falls. It is often the first day of the year for families to get out of doors and enjoy the new grass and budding trees, so it is also sometimes called the Walking on Green Grass Festival.

History

Although the Chinese have made it a practice to honor their ancestors since at least the time of the Shang Dynasty (1776–1122 B.C.), the Ching Ming Festival is believed to have begun during the Han Dynasty (206 B.C.–A.D. 221).

The great Chinese philosopher Confucius (551–479 B.C.) taught that people should "serve those now dead as if they were living." The teachings of Confucius are of major importance in Chinese culture. Confucianism, along with Taoism (pronounced TOW-izm) and Buddhism (pronounced BOO-dih-zem), is one of the major faiths in China.

The first celebrations of Ching Ming are thought to have included feasts, fairs, parades, and hunts. It was a time for playing games and flying kites and for enjoying the spring weather. Ching Ming was also a time for planting trees. It gradually evolved into a day for cleaning the graves of the ancestors, planting trees in cemeteries, and offering food and other gifts to the dead.

Folkore, Legends, Stories

Chinese literature is filled with stories about Ching Ming. Many of these stories and legends deal with death and the underworld and evil acts by spirits of the dead. Some tell how a person who did not receive a proper burial comes back as a vampire and tries to harm or kill anyone it meets. Others—such as the famous story "Mr. Li with the Iron Crutch"—tell how a part of the person's soul leaves his body and enters the body of another person.

In the story about Mr. Li, his ego, the part of the spirit that thinks and feels, leaves his body to travel to faraway places to visit with other spirits. The ego is gone for some time, and Mr. Li's family, believing he is dead, buries his body. When Mr. Li's ego returns, it cannot find its body and so inhabits the body of the first person it sees—a lame beggar with an iron crutch. Mr. Li's ego remains in the body of the beggar for the rest of his life.

The power of the willow

The willow tree, because it is one of the first trees to leaf in spring, is considered a symbol of new life and of power over darkness and evil. The Chinese often hang a sprig of willow over their doorways on Ching Ming to keep away evil spirits. Some also place a willow sprig in their hair and place willow branches beside family tombs to attract good spirits and drive away bad spirits and sickness.

Some people say that those who do not wear a willow sprig on Ching Ming will one day be reborn as a yellow dog. Chinese legend also holds that willow has the power to bring rain to help spring crops grow.

The tears of God

When spring rains fall at the same time as the Ching Ming Festival, they are said to be the tears of God, who weeps at the kindness of the people as they remember their ancestors. Rain is also said to be nature's way of joining people in mourning their dead.

These lines from an ancient Chinese poem written during the Tang Dynasty (618–907) show that this is an old belief:

> On Tomb Sweeping Day
> As the rain falls everywhere,
> People walking in the streets
> Feel the sorrow from within and without.

Legend of Cold Food Day

There lived a long time ago in the kingdom of Chin a loyal administrator named Chu. He was betrayed by fellow administrators and driven from the presence of the king. He journeyed to a mountain called Chinshan, surrounded by a forest, to live a life of solitude. When the king heard about this, he admired Chu's loyalty and searched for him throughout the kingdom. He finally learned that Chu was living in a cave on Chinshan mountain.

Chu would not come out of the cave, but the king so wanted to reward Chu that he had the forest set on fire to force his administrator out. Unfortunately, Chu suffocated in the cave. To honor his memory, people make no cooking fires on Ching Ming, and this day is known as Cold Food Day.

Customs, Traditions, Ceremonies

In traditional Chinese belief, dead family members are as much a part of the family as those who are alive. They are believed to exist in the "underworld," a place that is below the ground, much the same as the living do on earth, and so they still need things like food, money, and clothing. If the dead are provided with these things, they will in turn bless the living with prosperity and happiness.

When a person dies, his or her spirit can become good and helpful to living family members or mischievous and harmful, depending on how well the living take care of the deceased's spirit and honor his or her memory. Therefore, it is very important to perform the traditional rituals and ceremonies for the dead that are carried out on

Ching Ming and other special days. Such ceremonies include cleaning graves, preparing food for ancestors, and welcoming them to the family table. People also give ancestors offerings of money and new clothes, which are made of paper and burned so that their "essence," or spirit, can be used by the dead.

All ceremonies conducted during Ching Ming are held either at dusk or just before dawn, because night is believed to be the time when the dead are at rest in their graves.

Family reunions at Ching Ming

Because Ching Ming is a time for families—both living members and ancestors—to be reunited, Chinese people who live in other countries or in distant cities try to return to their homeland so that the entire family can celebrate together. To allow for travel, in many areas the festival is extended ten days before and after the actual date of Ching Ming.

Family members who cannot go home perform a ceremony wherever they are that includes filling a specially decorated paper bag with paper "money" and burning it on an altar containing fruit, flowers, and tea. They hope the "spirit" of the sacrifice will reach their ancestors.

Cleaning the tombs

Like Day of the Dead and All Souls' Day, Ching Ming is a time when Chinese families go to family cemeteries and spruce up the graves of their loved ones. This usually begins at dawn with a special ceremony that may include burning incense and shooting firecrackers. All family members, even children, help pull up weeds, clean tombstones and repaint the inscriptions, place fresh flowers and willow sprigs on the

"Ching Ming"

...Now light the grave fires.
Bring padded clothes,
grain, gifts, furniture;
sizzle the flames with wine
until warm spirits rise
to wake them from winter.

Our feet will soon begin
the summer journeys,
planting, harvesting.
Here are flowers and fire
for our ancestors;
from beneath the earth
may they be with us.

—*From "Ching Ming" by Irene Rawnsley*

Source: Let's Celebrate, *compiled by John Foster. Oxford: Oxford University Press, 1989, p. 40.*

graves, and perhaps plant new trees or shrubs. Yellow ribbons are also placed on the graves to keep away wandering ghosts who have no family to care for them.

Offerings for the ancestors

Once the graves are cleaned, families place offerings of food on stone altars or tables near the grave sites. The meals usually include meat, fruit and vegetables, wine, and the ancestor's favorite dishes. Paper money is placed on the graves and burned, in hopes that through the smoke the money will become real and can be used by the dead in the underworld. Some

Feeding the Hungry Ghosts

People of the Buddhist and Taoist (pronounced TOW-ist) religions in China, Vietnam, Taiwan, and other Far Eastern countries hold a month-long festival during July and August in honor of "hungry ghosts." These are the souls of people who died far away from their families, by violence, in war, or in accidents.

The Chinese believe these "hungry ghosts" are released from purgatory for one month each year to roam the earth. Purgatory is a place that is neither heaven nor hell, but is a holding area for souls of the dead. These souls are naked and hungry and need a taste of the world of the living before going back to the land of the dead. They must be well cared for, or they might cause trouble for the living.

Everyone makes or buys new clothes, play money, sports cars, horses, trains, and other objects—all made of paper. They burn the paper items in cemeteries, on roadsides, and in other places outside the homes, because it is unwise to invite the wandering souls inside. As the paper gifts rise up in smoke, the dead breathe them in for their use. The cars and other objects of transportation are thought to help carry souls to heaven. Celebrants also burn incense and offer prayers for the souls of the dead.

People prepare food for their dead relatives and often include three kinds of meat and five kinds of fruit. They place these offerings on the family altar. Puppet shows and a big feast are also held during the celebration. At the end of the Hungry Ghosts Festival, the spirits of the dead are sent home in paper boats on the waterways, with lighted candles to guide their way.

of the money even has "Issued by the Bank of the Underworld" or "Heaven Bank Note" printed on it.

After family members present their offerings, they may picnic on the food in the cemetery or take it home and have a feast, where they set places for the dead and expect them to visit and dine with them.

New clothes for the dead

The Chinese believe that the ancestors must be given a new suit of clothes during Ching Ming. They make these outfits out of paper, which are often packed in parcels, with the names of the ancestors who are to receive them written on the outside. Paper money is included in the parcels. A careful record of which ancestor is to receive which items is sometimes made.

The parcels are kept for a while in the homes, and the dead are invited to come and get them. Then the parcels are taken to the cemeteries and burned so they can reach the dead through the smoke. The ceremony is often accompanied by fireworks and burning candles and incense.

Ch'a Yeh Tan (Tea Eggs)

Ingredients

6 eggs

4 to 8 cups water, more or less as needed

2 tablespoons black tea leaves

1 tablespoon vinegar

½ tablespoon salt

1 teaspoon soy sauce

2 whole star anise (available at most supermarkets or Asian food stores)

Directions

1. Put eggs in small saucepan, cover with water, and bring to a roiling boil over medium-high heat. Reduce heat to simmer, and cook for 10 minutes.

2. Cool eggs under cold water and drain.

3. Using back of spoon, gently tap eggshells, making tiny cracks all over the surfaces. Do not peel; set aside.

4. In a small saucepan, combine tea leaves, vinegar, salt, soy sauce, star anise, and 3 cups water. Bring to a boil over high heat. Reduce heat to simmer, cover, and cook for 20 minutes.

5. Add cracked eggs to tea mixture, and simmer for about 15 minutes. Remove pan from heat and let eggs cool in liquid until cool enough to handle.

6. Remove eggs, carefully peel off shells, and discard liquid.

7. Serve tea eggs in a bowl or basket. Notice the pretty design on the egg whites. Tea eggs are eaten either at room temperature or chilled.

Source: Lois Sinaiko Webb. Holidays of the World Cookbook for Students. *Phoenix, Ariz.: Oryx Press, 1995, pp. 154–55.*

Foods, Recipes

Cooked meals are most often offered to the dead on Ching Ming, but some families keep an old custom called the Cold Food Feast. This custom comes from an ancient story that restricts the making of all household fires on the day before Ching Ming (see "Legend of Cold Food Day" under "Folklore, Legends, Stories"). Because people could not cook any food, they prepared cold meals that did not require cooking. This feast once lasted for three days. Today, people place foods such as uncooked rice and noodles and unpeeled fruit and vegetables on the graves.

Arts, Crafts, Games

During Ching Ming, Chinese families make elaborate paper offerings to ancestors. The offerings are burned during ceremonies in order to release their essence to the spirits. Paper models may include fancy houses, cars, beautiful clothing, jewelry, and other items treasured or wished for during life. Some of the more elaborate offerings may be five or six feet high and include amazing detail. Talented and skilled craftsmen work many hours to create these gifts for the dead, knowing they will all go up in smoke.

Kite-flying contests at Ching Ming

As a glorious day to enjoy the new spring weather, Ching Ming has traditionally been a good day for flying kites, an activity that began in ancient China. Today, after people clean the tombs and make offerings to the ancestors, they sometimes go to parks and fly beautifully made kites in many shapes and colors. Participating in kite-flying contests and watching kite exhibitions are popular ways to spend the spring afternoon.

Kite fliers from all over the world travel to China to compete in Ching Ming competitions. The kites may be painted with scenes from well-known Chinese legends or designed to perform stunts or create visual effects. Some make unusual sounds in the wind.

For More Information

Rosen, Mike. *Summer Festivals*. New York: Bookwright Press, 1991.

Snelling, John. *Buddhism*. New York: Bookwright Press, 1986.

Stepanchuk, Carol, and Charles Wong. *Mooncakes and Hungry Ghosts: Festivals of China*. San Francisco: China Books & Periodicals, 1991.

Web sites

"The Chinese Festivals." [Online] http://www.baxter.net/edunet/cat/chinafest/chinesef.html (accessed on February 8, 2000).

"The Qing Ming Festival." [Online] http://www.insidechina.com/culture/festival/qingming.php3 (accessed on February 15, 2000).

Japan

Name of Holiday: Obon Festival

Introduction

In Japan, an ancient and important Buddhist festival called the Obon, or Bon, Festival is celebrated in honor of deceased family members and ancestors. Buddhism (pronounced BOO-dih-zem) is one of the major religions of Asia and is one of the five largest in the world. Buddhism was founded by Prince Siddhartha Gautama (pronounced sid-DAR-tuh GOW-tuh-muh; c. 563–c. 483 B.C.), who was later given the name Buddha. His teachings form the foundation of Buddhism. Over ninety-six million people in Japan are Buddhist.

The Obon Festival is usually celebrated from August 13 to August 15, but in some places it is held from July 13 to July 15. Many people take a holiday from work during Obon, and businesses are usually closed.

History

The Obon Festival has been celebrated in Japan for about 1,400 years. The festival originated with the Buddhists in India, and with the spread of Buddhism it arrived in Japan during the early seventh century. The festival began when Buddhist priests celebrating a feast offered a share of the food to their ancestors. In Japan, only the families of noblemen celebrated the feast at first, but later everyone participated.

Folklore, Legends, Stories

According to Buddhist belief, if the living do not remember and pray for the dead, the souls of the dead will suffer greatly. Buddhists also believe that deceased ancestors continue to love and care for their living descendants even after death. It is said that during the Obon Festival the souls of the dead return to the land of the living from faraway mountains and from their graves. People once believed the souls returned from a place that lay beyond the sea.

Buddhists have a term for all the spirits of the dead combined into one, "O Shorai Sama." According to legend, this being comes riding on a snow-white horse on the first evening of the Obon Festival and leaves again at the close of the festival, when families place lanterns and food offerings on the rivers to be carried out to sea.

Customs, Traditions, Ceremonies

In the days before the Obon Festival, families clean their houses thoroughly, make any needed repairs, put fresh flowers in vases, and arrange everything as neatly as possible. Then they turn their attention to the family shrine, an altar or table-like stand that holds a statue of Buddha and tablets that name family ancestors. All the items are dusted and cleaned. Then a woven grass mat is placed on the floor in front of the shrine. The family's ancestor tablets are arranged on the mat as a welcome to the spirits, who will live in the shrine while they are visiting.

Lighting the welcoming fires

At dusk on the first evening of the Obon Festival, each family lights a small bonfire outside the entrance to their home to welcome the returning spirits. Throughout the festival, lights and lanterns are kept burning to help the spirits find their way. Families visit cemeteries during Obon and often leave lanterns burning at the grave sites of departed relatives. At the close of the festival, a farewell bonfire is lit at each home.

A bright farewell

At midnight on the last day of the Obon Festival, when it is time for the visiting spirits to return to the land of the dead, the Japanese perform a beautiful ceremony called Toro Nagashi (pronounced TORE-oh nah-GOSH-ee; floating paper lantern). The grass mat that was placed in front of the family shrine at the beginning of the festival is removed. Farewell rice dumplings, any leftover festival food, and the shrine decorations are placed on the mat. The sides of the mat are then folded together to create a bundle.

The bundle is placed on a small straw boat about three feet long, with a paper lantern fastened to the bow. The names of the dead who were honored are also placed inside the boats. Every family then walks to the waterfront and places their boat in the river, which becomes a sea of little lantern lights drifting toward the "unknown land," taking the spirits home.

Rice Dumplings

Ingredients

1⅓ cups glutinous (gluey) rice

¾ cup water chestnuts

canola oil spray

8 shiitake mushrooms, soaked in hot water for 20 minutes, stems removed, caps minced

1½ tablespoons peeled and minced fresh ginger

1 tablespoon minced green onion

3 tablespoons soy sauce

1 teaspoon Asian sesame oil

2 tablespoons cornstarch

Directions

1. Wash and drain the rice several times until the water runs clear. Drain and transfer to a baking sheet. Set aside.
2. Drop the water chestnuts into boiling water for 10 seconds. Drain. Rinse with cold water, drain, and chop.
3. Line 1 or 2 steamer trays with wax or parchment paper (or use aluminum pie plates punched with holes) and lightly brush with the oil.
4. Put the mushrooms, water chestnuts, ginger, green onion, soy sauce, sesame oil, and cornstarch in a bowl and stir to combine thoroughly.
5. Shape the mixture into balls about 1 inch in diameter. Roll each ball in the glutinous rice until well coated with grains, lightly pressing the rice into the ball so it sticks.
6. Place the balls on the steamer tray, leaving a ½-inch space between them.
7. Fill a large pot with water for steaming and bring it to a boil.
8. Stack the steamer trays over the boiling water or place 1 pie plate of dumplings on a stand over the boiling water. Cover and steam over high heat for 10 minutes or until the rice is cooked.
9. Serve hot with a dipping sauce made from soy sauce with a little vinegar and sesame oil added.

Clothing, Costumes

It is customary for everyone to get new clothes for Obon and to wear them during the festival. A special lightweight cotton *kimono* (pronounced kuh-MOH-noh; a long robe with wide sleeves, worn with a wide sash or belt) is the traditional costume worn for the Bon-Odori, the Japanese folk dancing held during the Obon Festival. This summer kimono is called the *yukata* (pronounced yuh-COT-uh), and is worn by both children and adults. Dancers often carry large fans during the dance.

Foods, Recipes

Like the Day of the Dead in Mexico, the Obon Festival is a time for welcoming the returning dead with many of the foods they enjoyed in life. The spirits are believed to be weary and hungry when they return from "the otherworld."

On the first night of the Obon Festival, family members place a meal of vegetables, fruits, and rice cakes near the family's altar, which is located inside the home. Buddhists do not eat meat on this occasion because it is a tradition to refrain from taking life during Obon. The family then invites their deceased relatives to join in the meal. During the three days of the festival, family members eat with and carry on conversations with their ancestors as if they were alive. Special rice dumplings are prepared on the last day of the festival to send the spirits on their way.

Arts, Crafts, Games

Decorating the family shrine for the Obon Festival is an occasion to put artistic talent to work. Favorite vegetables such as eggplants and cucumbers are carved into animal shapes, with grasses, leaves, and stems used for ornamentation. Long pasta noodles are also used for decoration.

Music, Dance

On the last night of Obon, the Japanese celebrate with folk dances called Bon-Odori, "Dance of Rejoicing." People dance by the light of paper or plastic lanterns, either on a wooden stage at an outdoor park or in a procession through the streets of town. The Bon-Odori are also performed in Buddhist temples, to the beat of a big drum called the *taiko* (pronounced TIE-koh).

Some of the dances are more like Western folk dances, but others are traditional Japanese dances, with graceful movements and postures, spinning, and hand clapping. The dancers usually perform to music played from a recording, but the more elaborate Bon-Odori also include live musicians and puppet shows. The traditional music features drums and flutes.

The Bon-Odori was once a more solemn dance, performed by family members who were in mourning for a lost one. Now it is a dance to welcome and comfort the returning ancestors and to bring joy to the living.

Special Role of Children, Young Adults

One reason for honoring the ancestors during Obon is to help children remember their heritage and to encourage them to show respect for parents, grandparents, and other adult relatives. Therefore, children participate in most aspects of the Obon Festival. They often help make decorations for the family shrine, help prepare food, and visit the graves. Children love the Bon-Odori folk dances and are sometimes treated afterward to ice cream or candy. They also like to buy small lanterns at the Bon-Odori dances. In some places, gifts are given during the Obon Festival.

For More Information

MacMillan, Diane. *Japanese Children's Day and the Obon Festival.* Springfield, N.J.: Enslow Publishers, 1997.

Suyenaga, Ruth. *Obon (Multicultural Celebrations).* Cleveland: Modern Curriculum Press, 1993.

Mexico

Name of Holiday: El Día de los Muertos; Day iof the Dead

Introduction

One of the most popular holidays in Mexico is El Día de Los Muertos (pronounced el DEE-a day los MWAIR-tose), or the Day of the Dead. It is a three-day celebration that takes place on October 31, November 1 (All Saints' Day), and November 2 (All Souls' Day). The Day of the Dead is a time for celebrating death and for honoring the dead. During this period, the spirits of all those who have died are believed to return to their earthly homes, where they are made welcome with food, flowers, and gifts.

From noon on October 31 until noon on November 1, the spirits of infants and young children who have died—called *difuntos chiquitos* (pronounced dee-FOON-tose chee-KEY-tose)—are said to return. This day is often referred to as Día de los Angelitos (Day of the Little Angels) or Día de los Niños, meaning Day of the Children.

The spirits of adults who have died are believed to return from noon on November 1 until the evening of November 2. This day is often called Día de los Difuntos, or Day of the Faithful Dead. The night

of November 1, when the living keep watch and pray at the graves of their deceased family members, is called Noche de los Muertos, or Night of the Dead.

History

The Day of the Dead is an ancient holiday in Mexico. Its origins can be traced back to the Aztec Indians, ancestors of many modern-day Mexicans, who ruled central Mexico from the 1300s to 1520. During a month-long harvest celebration held at the end of summer, the Aztecs honored the dead. The festivities were presided over by their god of death, Mictlantecuhtli (pronounced meek-tlan-teh-KOOH-tlee). As part of the celebrations, many prisoners taken in war were sacrificed to the blood-thirsty Aztec sun god and god of war, Huitzilopochtli (pronounced weet-zeel-oh-POKE-tlee). The skulls of the dead were arranged on racks in the temples.

In 1521, the Aztecs were conquered by Spain. As the Spanish began to colonize Mexico, Spanish missionaries introduced the region to Roman Catholicism. Over time, the Aztec beliefs about the honor of death and the land of the dead combined with the Christian practice of remembering the saints on All Saints' Day (November 1) and the dead on All Souls' Day (November 2).

Folklore, Legends, Stories

Some native peoples of Mexico and Latin America believe they continue to have a relationship with people they are close to, who have died. For them, the line between the earthly world and the spirit world is blurred, and they view death as an integral part of life. This makes for an attitude toward death that is very different from that found in other cultures. Much of Latin American literature includes these themes of death and the afterlife.

An example is the book *One Hundred Years of Solitude,* written in 1967 by the famous modern-day Latin American writer Gabriel García Márquez (1928–). In the story, several characters continue to act in the world of the living after they have died and left their physical bodies.

Readings and performances

During Day of the Dead festivals, many towns sponsor readings and performances of works that deal with death or visits by spirits. Sometimes there are contests with prizes for the best skit. The skits are simple dramatizations of a story or joke about tricking or being tricked by death. One of the most popular plays presented throughout Mexico during El Día de Los Muertos is *Don Juan Tenorio,* written in 1844 by Spanish poet José Zorrilla y Moral (1817–1893).

Don Juan Tenorio: Don Juan has been a legendary hero in folklore since the 1600s. Stories about him began in Spain, and several well-known playwrights wrote versions of the Don Juan legend. The great composer Wolfgang Amadeus Mozart (1756–1791) wrote the opera *Don Giovanni* about Don Juan in 1787, and composer Richard Strauss (1864–1914) wrote his symphonic poem *Don Juan* in 1889.

Don Juan is a hero who is both comical and tragic. He chases many women but can never find the perfect one, and his search always destroys him. In the original Spanish version of the play, Don Juan wins

Spirits That Fly Home

The Aztecs believed that when certain people died, their spirits flew to a special world as birds and butterflies. These included persons sacrificed to the gods, women who died in childbirth, and warriors. Because of this belief, Aztecs carved many butterfly images on their monuments. For hundreds of years, people in Mexico have thought that the monarch butterflies, which return to central Mexico each year in October from their summer homes in the United States and Canada, carry the returning spirits of the dead.

the love of the daughter of the commander of Seville (a city in Spain) and then kills her father in a duel because the father disapproves of their love. Don Juan later invites a statue of the commander to a feast as a joke, but the statue comes to life and drags Don Juan down to hell.

The play *Don Juan Tenorio* was first performed on the Day of the Dead in 1864. Since then, it has become a Mexican tradition to see the play during Day of the Dead festivities, which is not difficult because performances take place all over Mexico. In Zorrilla's version of the story, Don Juan is not taken to hell. His soul is saved by the love of a young woman, Doña Ines, who has died. Her spirit comes back to rescue Don Juan as he confesses his sins and asks for mercy in a cemetery, with skeletons and ghosts trying to grab him and take him to hell.

On the lighter side

Not all literary works associated with the Day of the Dead are dark and foreboding. Many have been created to help people face a subject that is otherwise frightening and sad. This humorous poem that was popular in the early 1900s in Mexico shows the lighter side of El Día de Los Muertos:

> This happy skull
> today invites all mortals
> to come on a visit to the infernal
> regions.
> There'll be special trains
> for your enjoyment on this trip
> and there's no need to dress up for it.

Customs, Traditions, Ceremonies

As the time for the spirits of the dead to return approaches, festival preparations increase. People in rural areas go into towns carrying bundles of marigolds and other flowers that will be used to decorate graves and family altars. The windows of bakeries and other shops fill up with breads in the shape of skulls and skeletons. People are busy buying spices and colorful chilies and other ingredients for making the deceased's favorite foods and beverages. They also purchase candles, incense burners, and the latest Halloween masks.

Decorating the graves

Family members of the deceased make an annual pilgrimage to cemeteries before the Day of the Dead to clean and repair tombstones, crosses, and crypts; pull up weeds; and decorate the graves with colored paper streamers, flowers, candles, and other beautiful ornaments. They also paint the grave markers and crypts in bright pinks, yellows, and blues.

Preparing the *ofrendas*

Day of the Dead ceremonies vary according to region, but in many homes they begin with a candlelight vigil. An elaborate altar is prepared to welcome the spirits of the dead. The altar is decorated with photographs of the departed family members and with *ofrendas* (pronounced off-FREN-das), or offerings. These offerings often include objects made from sugar, such as small animals, miniature plates of food, small coffins with pop-up skeletons, and skulls. They might also include toys and candy for deceased children, cigarettes for those who smoked in life, new clothes, beads, and incense.

Many candles are lit, and a path of "flowers of the dead" (yellow marigolds) is strewn from outside the home to the altar to help the dead find their way. Often a bowl of clean water and a towel are provided so that the spirits can refresh themselves after their journey.

Mexicans believe that the dead warm their cold hands over the candle flames, and the burning incense keeps away evil spirits and blesses the food on the altar. The spirits of the dead eat only the "essence," or aroma, of the food. The actual food is eaten by the living after the spirits have gone back to their graves, on November 3.

On the evening of October 31, friends and neighbors visit homes where the family has lost a child in the past year. They take special toys for the child's spirit to play with and sweet treats for the *angelito* (soul of the dead child). Visitors come the following day to honor adults who have

Crucifixes, candles, flowers, food, and other offerings decorate this family altar for the Day of the Dead, when the spirits of all those who have died are believed to return to their earthly homes.
Reproduced by permission of the Corbis Corporation (Bellevue).

died during the year. If a person died by accident or by violent or criminal means, Day of the Dead offerings are placed outside the home to keep unpardoned spirits from entering.

Keeping watch for the spirits

On the night of November 1, when the spirits of adults who have died are said to return to the land of the living, families go to cemeteries to await the arrival of the

A musician sings songs at the graves of Montalvo family members on November 1, 1999, in Mexico City, Mexico. On the night of November 1, many families go to cemeteries to await the arrival of the spirits of their loved ones. Reproduced by permission of AP/Wide World Photos.

spirits of their loved ones. There they set up food and other items from their home altars, burn candles, pray, weep, and keep watch through the night as the dead return.

This occasion, however, is not solemn for everyone. Food and drink is usually available, and outside the cemeteries children play, men visit, and teens listen to music. Many people leave the cemeteries at midnight, when church bells toll to call the spirits back to the land of the dead. Some stay until dawn, when a priest offers prayers for the souls of the dead, ending the all-night watch.

Northern customs not always welcome

Although Halloween and the Day of the Dead evolved separately, they are close cousins, sharing some of the same symbols and falling at the same time of year. In recent years, North American and British Halloween customs have filtered into the Mexican celebration of the Day of the Dead. Part of the reason for this is the passing of the North American Free Trade Agreement (NAFTA), which has increased trade among these countries.

Many Mexican children can now buy Halloween trick-or-treat costumes, plastic jack-o'-lanterns, witches' hats, and rubber masks. They have also taken up the Halloween trick-or-treating custom. As they pass through the streets before and during Day of the Dead, they shout "Calaveras!" ("Skulls!") instead of "trick or treat!" People often give them money instead of candy; families sometimes use the money to offset the cost of food and decorations purchased for the Day of the Dead celebrations.

The same trend is moving southward into the Central American countries of Honduras, Guatemala, Nicaragua, and Costa Rica, where the traditional Catholic holidays All Saints' Day and All Souls' Day are now being celebrated with "Witches' Night" or Halloween activities like trick-or-treating. Stores have begun to decorate for Halloween, with jack-o'-lanterns and black cats appearing next to skulls and skeletons in window displays. Costume parties are also held.

Such Halloween celebrations are growing every year, even though the Catholic Church frowns on them. Many adults do not like it that Halloween is competing with Day of the Dead among young people, so they are increasing activities and displays in public places to promote the traditional Mexican Day of the Dead customs.

Clothing, Costumes

Dressing in costumes, or mumming, plays a significant part in Mexico's Day of the Dead festivities. On the nights of October 31 and November 1, male mummers called *comparsas* (pronounced kome-PAR-sus) parade through town and walk from house to house performing comic skits about politicians or other personalities. They are rewarded with money and drinks. There are also contests for the best *calavera* (skull) costumes.

The mummers are followed by crowds of onlookers, who cheer and applaud their lighthearted skits. Children wearing Halloween costumes and masks and carrying jack-o'-lanterns also join the fun and make a little mischief. Some even invent stories about creatures from beyond the grave to tell to people in the crowd. For their efforts, the children collect money and treats.

Foods, Recipes

The Day of the Dead is an occasion for preparing lots of food in Mexico. In town, the bakeries fill their windows with pastries made in the shapes of death: skulls, coffins, little human figures, skeletons, and bones. Painted loaves of bread and *pan de muerto* (bread of the dead) are also sold. Pan de muerto is made in small round loaves and decorated with pieces of dough in the form of tears or bones.

When visiting cemeteries, families often take a picnic basket containing pan de muerto along with other colorful offerings such as chocolate and yellow marigolds. The Day of the Dead is not only an occasion to make offerings to the spirits, it is also a time for feasting. The delicious dishes once favored by the dead are shared with friends and neighbors after the spirits have partaken of the food's "essence."

Arts, Crafts, Games

The symbol most associated with El Día de Los Muertos is the skeleton. Shops everywhere in Mexico display skeletons in

Pan de Muerto (Bread of the Dead)

Ingredients

½ cup butter, melted

¼ cup lukewarm water

4 cups all-purpose flour

1 teaspoon dry yeast

½ cup sugar

6 eggs

1 teaspoon salt

2 teaspoons aniseed

1 teaspoon ground nutmeg

1 teaspoon orange extract

Directions

1. Combine ½ cup of the flour with the yeast and the lukewarm water. Set aside until it doubles in volume.

2. Meanwhile, in a large mixing bowl place the remaining flour, making a well in the center. Pour the eggs, sugar, salt, aniseed, and nutmeg in the well.

3. Beat ingredients together thoroughly, then add the yeast mixture and combine. Knead dough on a lightly floured board until smooth and elastic, about 5 to 10 minutes.

4. Lightly grease a bowl and place dough in it. Cover with plastic wrap, and let rise in warm, draft-free area about 2 hours or until doubled in size.

5. Punch the dough down and shape into round loaves with "crossbones" placed for decoration around the top. To make crossbones, roll an egg-size piece of dough between the palms of your hands and form a rope about 8 inches long. Cut the rope into 2 equal pieces and place them in the form of an X on top of the loaves. Let these loaves rise for 1 hour.

6. Bake loaves in a preheated 350 degree oven for 40 minutes. Remove from oven.

7. To make glaze, mix ⅔ cup sugar, ½ cup orange juice, and 2 tablespoons grated orange peel in a saucepan. Bring to a boil and simmer for 2 minutes. Apply glaze to the loaves of pan de muerto with a pastry brush and sprinkle with sugar if desired.

all shapes and sizes. There are dancing skeletons with springs that make arms, legs, and skulls bounce up and down; skeletons dressed in every kind of clothing and representing probably every occupation, such as bony farmers and schoolteachers, secretaries and musicians; and skeletons acting out scenes from everyday life. These hand-made Day of the Dead figurines are called *calacas* (pronounced kah-LOCK-uhs).

Decorating the sun, moon, and stars

A special trellis called an *arco* is prepared by the men and young boys of Janitzio Island in northwestern Mexico, which is said to hold the most exotic and beautiful Day of the Dead ceremony. Tourists come from many countries to view the celebrations, especially the candlelight vigil at the island's cemetery.

The arco is made from wooden sticks. It is first covered with yellow marigolds, the traditional flowers of the dead, by using fishing line to tie them to the sticks. Then fruits like apples, oranges, and bananas are tied on, followed by shaped loaves of pan de muerto, sugar skulls, and lots of other candies in the shape of animals, angels, brides and grooms, and even Coca-Cola bottles. Dog-shaped candies are especially popular because dogs are good companions and make excellent guides for the dead. The arco represents the heavens and planets, sun, moon, and stars. It also represents the resting place of the dead and the gifts of life.

The arcos are carried to the cemetery along with the many other gifts for the dead: food, flowers, candles, and incense. They are set up at the center of each grave site and glow in candlelight throughout the night. Women and children sit all night, giving warmth and companionship to the dead. The men linger on the outskirts of the graveyard, sipping tequila or other beverages and singing *alabanzas,* or hymns to the dead.

When the dawn comes up over Lake Patzcuaro (pronounced potz-KWAH-row), the women open their baskets laden with food, offer them to heaven, to the souls of the dead, and then to each other. Well-fed and happy, the celebrants leave the cemetery at daybreak.

Artful tissue banners

In the village of San Salvador Huix-colotla (pronounced WEES-koh-loht-luh),

Sugar Skulls

Ingredients

2 cups powdered (confectioner's) sugar
⅓ cup cornstarch
1 tablespoon light corn syrup
½ teaspoon vanilla extract
1 egg white
food coloring and small paintbrush

Directions

1. Stir together the egg white, corn syrup, and vanilla in a bowl and then slowly add the sugar, while continuing to stir. Mix well.

2. Sprinkle cornstarch onto your work surface to keep the sugar mixture from sticking as you form it into a ball.

3. Make skulls or other shapes from small pieces of the sugar ball, using cornstarch to keep the pieces from sticking to your hands or the work surface.

4. When the skulls are dry, use a paintbrush to paint them with food coloring.

5. You may make the sugar ball ahead of time and save it by wrapping it tightly in plastic and keeping it in the refrigerator until you are ready to use it.

artisans are famous for their carefully cut tissue banners, which are displayed to welcome the spirits of the dead. Designs are cut into as many as fifty sheets of tissue paper at a time, using more than fifty different *fierritos* (tiny chisels), each making its own distinct cut.

Traditional patterns for people living in the countryside are angels, crosses, and birds, but in Mexico City, the most popular are skeletons engaged in various activities. Colored tissue banners are displayed on October 31 and November 1 for the return of the children who have died. On the following day, black and white banners are displayed for the return of the spirits of deceased adults.

For More Information

Beimler, Rosalind Rosoff. *The Days of the Dead (Los Días de Los Muertos)*. San Francisco: Collins, 1991.

Carmichael, Elizabeth, and Chloë Sayer. *The Skeleton at the Feast: The Day of the Dead in Mexico.* Austin: University of Texas Press, 1991.

Sayer, Chloë. *The Mexican Day of the Dead.* Boston: Shambhala, 1990.

Web sites

"Celebration on Sacred Soil." [Online] http://www.indetroit.com/allmedia/dead/default.htm (accessed on February 9, 2000).

"Los Dias de los Muertos: Celebrating the Mexican Holiday The Days of the Dead." [Online] http://www.holidays.net/halloween/muertos.htm (accessed on February 9, 2000).

Palfrey, Dale Hoyt. "The Day of the Dead: Mexico Honors Those Gone But Not Forgotten." *Mexico Connect*, 1995. [Online] http://www.mexconnect.com/mex_/muertos.html (accessed on February 9, 2000).

United Kingdom

Name of Holiday: Halloween

Introduction

The celebration of Halloween originated in parts of the United Kingdom with the ancient Celts (pronounced KELTS), who believed that spirits roamed the earth on this night. People especially in Ireland, Scotland, and Wales observed the holiday, and Irish immigrants are said to have brought Halloween traditions to the United States. Many old folk customs are still carried out in parts of the United Kingdom, but Halloween trick-or-treating in the cities closely resembles the U.S. version.

History

Halloween is one of the most important holidays in Ireland, Scotland, and Wales. It is believed to have begun more than two thousand years ago with the Celtic festival of Samhain (pronounced SOW-en), which means "summer's end." Samhain was celebrated to end the harvest and to welcome the winter. This turning point in the year was considered a magical time that opened the door to the dead and allowed ghosts and spirits into the world. Since then, Halloween has been linked with the dead and with the realm of witches, ghosts, elves, fairies, and other supernatural beings.

Because the spirit world was open, Halloween became the perfect time for predicting the future. It was also a time for young pranksters to make mischief, especially in farming communities, and blame it on the spirits believed to roam on Halloween night. They took gates off their hinges, whitewashed windows, hid livestock, and even chained all the house doors so no one could get out.

Halloween was probably not widely celebrated in England before the early 1900s. It was thus little known in England's American colonies other than as a commemoration of the Christian All Saints' Day. This began to change when Irish immigrants brought their Halloween customs and traditions to America in the middle 1800s. With them, the Irish brought an observance of Halloween that blended with American customs to eventually become the major celebration it is today.

"Guising" (pronounced GUY-zing), or dressing in disguise, was replaced by dressing up as ghosts, witches, and goblins. Turnip lanterns became jack-o'-lanterns, and mischief making became trick-or-treating. The same process occurred in England, partly because of the Irish living there and partly because of increasing American cultural influence. By the middle of the twentieth century, Halloween had become a major festival in many parts of England. Today, it is a favorite national folk holiday just as it is in the United States.

Folklore, Legends, Stories

Folktales and superstitions about ghosts, witches, fairies, and ghoulies exist in every country in the United Kingdom. They are passed on from generation to generation to try to explain the unexplainable. The tales also travel from country to country as people move from one place to the next. The tradition is so great in these countries that Wales, Ireland, Scotland, and England have produced some of the world's best storytellers.

The keyhole ghosts

In Wales, the name for All Hallows' Eve is Nos Galan Gaeaf. It is an important holiday with many superstitions attached to it. Welsh legends say that ghosts of the dead appear at midnight on All Hallows' Eve. In some areas of Wales, a brave village youth would go into the churchyard, where these ghosts were believed to be walking about. He would put his finger over the keyhole of the church door to keep spirits from escaping. Some people believed that through the keyhole, the boy could see ghosts of those who would soon die.

An Irishman named Jack

An old Irish folktale about a man named Jack is the basis for the Halloween jack-o'-lantern. Jack was said to have made a pact with the devil so that the devil could never claim his soul. According to the legend, when Jack died he was refused entry into heaven. But when he went to the gates of hell, the devil could not allow him in either. Jack took a coal from the fires of hell, hollowed out a turnip, and placed the coal inside. Legend says this "lantern" still lights Jack's way as he wanders the earth until the end of time.

A similar story is about a character named Will o' the Wisp, who is thought to be a wandering spirit who roams through swamps and bogs. This story was invented to explain the mysterious lights that sometime appear in swampy areas. These lights are now thought to be gases released from decaying plant matter. Some say ugly faces

Carving jack-o'-lanterns is a custom that came from the British Isles, where children once carved lanterns from large turnips, gourds, and beets. Reproduced by permission of AP/Wide World Photos.

Famous Halloween poems by Robert Burns

Scottish national poet Robert "Robbie" Burns (1759–1796) wrote two long poems—"Halloween" and "Tam o' Shanter"—that contributed much to the development of Halloween as an important holiday. When Scottish immigrants came to America, they recited the poems on Halloween. As a result, many American Halloween traditions came from ideas taken from these works.

Burns's poems are written in "Scots," a dialect of northern Scotland spoken by nearly all Scottish people of his day. "Tam o' Shanter" is based on a witch story told about Alloway Kirk, an old ruin near Burns's home in Ayr, Scotland. Like the American story *The Legend of Sleepy Hollow,* by Washington Irving, "Tam o' Shanter" is about the midnight ride of a comic folk hero, Tam. Tam is chased by witches until he comes to a bridge. Horse and rider cross the bridge, leaving the witches behind because witches will not cross water. Just at the last moment, a witch snatches the tail off Tam's mare.

In the poem "Halloween," Burns writes about many of the traditional Halloween customs of his day, such as pulling the kale, playing the game the Three Luggies, and burning nuts on the hearth to determine a sweetheart's faithfulness (see "Customs, Traditions, Ceremonies" and "Arts, Crafts, Games").

were carved on jack-o'-lanterns to frighten such evil spirits away.

A tunic for your life

The Scottish believed that a person who took a three-legged stool and sat at the intersection of three roads at midnight on Halloween would see fairies. These fairies would speak the names of persons who were going to die during the year. If the brave soul took articles of clothing and threw them to the fairies, the fairies would be pleased and prevent the person from dying.

Customs, Traditions, Ceremonies

Many of the Halloween customs still practiced today in the United Kingdom began hundreds of years ago. One tradition that has remained is playing games or performing rituals that will foretell the future. In many of these rituals, young people try to predict, or "divine," whom they will marry. Other traditions that continue to play a part in Halloween festivities are dressing in costume and trick-or-treating.

Nutcrack Night in Ireland

An old folk custom in Ireland once gave the name Nutcrack Night to Halloween. When a young woman wanted to know if her boyfriend was faithful, she put three nuts on the bars of the fireplace grate, naming one nut for herself and the others for two boyfriends. If a nut cracked or jumped, the boy would prove unfaithful; if it began to blaze or burn, he liked the girl making the trial. If the nuts named after the girl and her boyfriend burned together, the couple would one day marry.

Pulling the kale

In another custom, "pulling the kail" (kale; cabbage), young people would go out hand in hand and blindfolded into the *kailyard,* or garden. Each one pulled up the first stalk of kale he or she encountered. They returned to the fireside to examine their stalks. Each person's stalk was said to reveal information about that person's future wife or husband. The amount of earth clinging to the stalk, for example, determined the size of the future mate's fortune or dowry; the taste of the pith, or core, indicated the person's temper.

In some areas, the cabbage's head was used to determine the appearance of a future husband. A closed white head meant the girl would marry an old man. An open

green head indicated a young man as the future groom.

"Please to help the guisers"

"Guising," or dressing in disguise, on All Hallows' Eve, has been a popular custom in Scotland for hundreds of years. It is sometimes called "galoshin." It began in about the sixteenth century and continued into the twentieth century. Guising is one of the customs that gave us the modern Halloween activity called trick-or-treating.

Groups of young men or children put on scary "false faces," or masks, and, as soon as it was dark, went through the village streets carrying turnip lanterns or torches made from kale stalks. They sang Halloween rhymes and gave small performances as they went from door to door, saying, "Please to help the guisers." People gave them apples, nuts, and sometimes coins. They often used any money received to buy fireworks for Halloween.

Early Halloween costumes in Wales

In the late nineteenth century in some parts of Wales, young people wore clothes of the opposite gender and went from house to house singing verses and riddles. In other places, men dressed in sheepskins and old ragged clothes masked their faces and went around calling themselves *gwrachod* (hags), much feared creatures in medieval Wales. They frightened children and were rude to adults and were eventually stopped by the police.

Thump-the-Door Night

On the Isle of Man in the early 1900s, boys would throw cabbages or turnips at doors until the homeowner came out and gave them money or a treat.

Because of this custom, Halloween was known as Thump-the-Door Night.

Welsh hillsides on fire and burning Guy Fawkes

In centuries past, families lit Halloween bonfires on hillsides to see whose bonfire would burn longest. They roasted potatoes and apples in the fire and danced around or jumped over the flames. Each person chose a stone and threw it into the fire. The next morning, when the fire was out, they would go back to look for their stones. It was good luck to find the stone, bad luck if it could not be found.

Today on Halloween, people may still light bonfires in rural areas, but most bonfires are reserved for Guy Fawkes Day, celebrated on November 5. The night of Guy Fawkes Day is called Bonfire Night, and people throughout the United Kingdom light bonfires and burn lifelike representations of Guy Fawkes. In 1605, Fawkes was involved in a plot with other Englishmen to blow up the British Houses of Parliament in revenge for laws against Catholics. This Gunpowder Plot was discovered, and Fawkes was arrested and executed. Since the mid-1850s, burning a figure of Guy Fawkes has become an annual tradition.

Putting the torch to witches and ghosts

In early Scotland, people often lit peat torches and carried them through orchards to burn any witches that might be lurking about. It was commonly believed that witches and ghosts feared fire, so the torches were believed to be a powerful weapon against them. In the Scottish Highlands, farmers would carry lighted torches into the fields on Halloween and walk clockwise around the fields, believing that this custom would ensure a good year for crops. It was later considered bad luck to allow a fire to go out on All Hallows' Eve.

Clothing, Costumes

The tradition of dressing in costume on Halloween may have begun with the Celts in pre-Christian England, Scotland, Ireland, and Wales. Some writers say the Celts wore animal skins and other disguises during the celebration of Samhain so that evil spirits would not recognize them.

Later traditions include those of the mummers, who dressed in costumes and performed from house to house on many holidays. The British guisers wore costumes and masks to disguise themselves on their outings around town. Today, children and adults dress as ghosts (called ghoulies or kelpies in Scotland), witches, vampires, and skeletons. In most areas, children go trick-or-treating for candy and other treats on Halloween, much the same as children in the United States and other countries do.

Foods, Recipes

Colcannon is the favorite traditional Irish Halloween dish. It is made from potatoes, turnips, parsnips, cabbage, onions, and other fall harvest vegetables. It is sometimes used to foretell the future by placing tokens inside it, such as a ring, a coin, a miniature doll, and a thimble. When the colcannon is dished out, the person who gets the ring is supposed to marry; the one who finds the doll is expected to have children; the one who gets the thimble will remain single; and the one who

Colcannon

Ingredients

6 potatoes, peeled and cut into quarters

6 tablespoons butter or margarine

½ cup milk, or more if needed

6 green onions, washed, trimmed, and chopped fine

salt and pepper to taste

4 cups chopped green cabbage

Directions

1. Put potatoes into a medium saucepan and cover with water. Bring to a boil over high heat, then reduce heat to medium. Cover and cook until soft, about 20 minutes.

2. Drain potatoes and transfer to a large mixing bowl.

3. Add 2 tablespoons of the butter or margarine and ½ cup milk. Mash the potatoes until fluffy. Add more milk if needed.

4. Add green onions and salt and pepper to taste, stirring well. Set potatoes aside.

5. Melt 4 tablespoons butter or margarine in a large skillet over medium-high heat. Add cabbage and stir.

6. Reduce heat to simmer, cover, and cook for about 15 minutes, or until cabbage is tender.

7. Add potato mixture to cabbage in skillet, stir, and dot top of colcannon with about 4 or 5 teaspoons of butter or margarine.

8. Cover and heat through over medium-low heat for about 10 minutes. Serve warm.

receives the coin will be wealthy. This custom is still carried out at some Halloween parties today.

Spooning the crowdie

Crowdie was a popular Halloween dish in Great Britain during the Middle Ages, or medieval times (about 500 to 1500). Like colcannon, it was used to predict the future. It was made from whipped sweet cream mixed with apple sauce and had six items—two rings, two marbles, and two coins—placed inside for six players. Using spoons, players ate crowdie directly from a large dish. The players who found the rings would soon marry; those who discovered coins would be wealthy; and those who got marbles would remain single. If a player spooned up only crowdie, his or her life would be full of sweet surprises.

Barmbrack and sowens for Halloween

A traditional British Halloween food is barmbrack, a kind of bread with raisins and currants. A treat is placed inside the bread and is said to predict the finder's future. A person who finds a ring will soon wed; a piece of straw indicates a prosperous year. Another popular dish at Halloween is sowens, a porridge made from the husks of oatmeal.

Arts, Crafts, Games

In Scotland, Halloween is associated with fun and revelry at the fireside. It is also associated with ceremonies by young people for divining their future sweetheart. In one such game, the Three Luggies, one bowl is filled with clean water, another with dirty water, and a third is left empty. The bowls are arranged on the hearth. A player is blindfolded and is told to dip his fingers into one of the bowls. If the person dips into the clean water, he is destined to marry; if the player dips into dirty water, he will be a widow or widower; if the player dips into the empty bowl, he or she will never marry. The Three Luggies is still a popular Halloween game.

Dooking and forking, snapping and peeling

Apples play a big role in Halloween traditions in Wales and Scotland. The most popular Halloween game is bobbing for apples, called "dooking fur aiples" in Scotland. A number of apples are placed in a large bowl or barrel of water set on the floor. Without using their hands, players try to pick up apples using only their teeth. The apples with stems are usually caught first, and then comes the quest for those with no stem. Some players actually suck up the smaller apples into their mouths. Others plunge their heads into the barrel of water, force an apple to the bottom, and then grab it with their teeth, emerging dripping wet.

Today, younger children in Scotland play "forkin' fur aiples," an easier

game. Each child stands on a chair and holds a fork, pointed downward over the apple barrel, in his or her teeth. If the fork skewers an apple when the child lets go, he or she gets to keep the apple.

Apple and Candle Night is the traditional name given to Halloween in the Swansea area of Wales. The game of Apple and Candle is played by suspending a stick from the ceiling, with an apple attached to one end and a candle to the other. The stick is then twirled rapidly, and players, without using their hands, try to grab the apple with their teeth as it spins around. They often end up with a mouthful of candle wax instead.

In another game, players peel an apple in a single piece and toss the peel over their shoulder. The letter of the alphabet the peel most resembles when it falls to the ground is the initial of the player's future husband or wife.

For More Information

Chambers, Catherine. *All Saints, All Souls, and Halloween.* Austin, Tex.: Raintree Steck-Vaughn, 1997.

Hintz, Martin, and Kate Hintz. *Halloween: Why We Celebrate It the Way We Do.* Mankato, Minn.: Capstone Press, 1996.

Web sites

"The Story of Halloween." [Online] http://www.scottishradiance.com/halstory.htm (accessed December 1999).

United States

Name of Holiday: Halloween

Introduction

In some areas of the United States, Halloween celebrations began as early as the 1800s. The tradition of trick-or-treating, however, did not spread throughout the nation until about the 1950s. Today, Halloween is a favorite folk holiday, and Americans spend nearly as much on Halloween costumes, decorations, and candy as they do at Christmas. Trick-or-treating is still popular with children, whereas adults enjoy decorating, going to costume parties, watching horror films, and participating in Halloween parades. Many children collect money for the United Nations Children's Fund (UNICEF) on their trick-or-treating rounds. UNICEF is an international organization that works to protect the rights of children.

National Magic Day

October 31 has also been proclaimed National Magic Day in the United States in honor of famous illusionist and escape artist Harry Houdini (1874–1926), who died on October 31, 1926. Houdini, whose real name was Ehrich Weiss, was an authority on magic and was fascinated by spiritualism. Spiritualism is the belief that the dead can communicate with the living. He spent a great part of his later life attending seances and exposing the tricks of mediums, who claimed they could help people speak with the dead. Houdini left his extensive library of books about magic to the U.S. Library of Congress.

History

With the immigration of more than seven million people from countries all over the world during the middle 1800s, the United States became a melting pot of beliefs about the occult and ways of celebrating the harvest season. The Irish, who came in large numbers because of a famine in their country, had a particularly strong influence on the celebration of Halloween as a folk holiday.

While Irish boys and young men went from house to house in disguises, chanting and asking for bread or treats, girls and women stayed home and divined, or predicted, the identity of their future husbands. The Irish also discovered in the native New World pumpkin great possibilities for making Halloween lanterns to guide them about on Halloween night. Thus began the custom of carving jack-o'-lanterns as it is done today.

In the early 1900s, the towns of Anoka, Minnesota, and Allentown, Pennsylvania, hosted some of the first public Halloween celebrations and parades in the United States. With the early twentieth century also came a renewal of Halloween mischief making. Pranksters knocked over outhouses, broke windows, and turned in false fire alarms. They threw eggs, soaped windows, and disabled streetcars by disengaging trolley wires. Such activities were later curtailed by community and school groups.

World War II (1939–45) also slowed Halloween mischief, and after the war the holiday's focus changed to one of a wholesome folk holiday for children. During the 1950s and 1960s, dressing in costumes and trick-or-treating for candy reached the height of their popularity.

Since then, many schools and churches have turned away from supernatural Halloween themes and have started to organize parties and fairs for children along seasonal, historical, or religious themes. What was once a Halloween carnival is now a fall festival, and children dress in costumes on themes unrelated to the supernatural.

Folklore, Legends, Stories

Immigrants who came to the United States brought with them tales of ghosts and goblins, witches and fairies. Many of the tales, such as the legend of the jack-o'-lantern, contributed to Halloween customs and rituals that are still practiced today. These stories also influenced American authors. One writer who sprang from this supernatural tradition was Washington Irving.

The Legend of Sleepy Hollow

The Legend of Sleepy Hollow (1820), by American author Washington Irving (1783–1859), is a Halloween tale that shows how a belief in spirits thrived in early America. The people of Sleepy Hollow tell endless tales of witches, ghosts, and goblins, including a story about the Headless Horseman, the ghost of a soldier whose head was blown off by a cannonball. He is said to roam through the hollow each night on his steed, looking for his missing head, then gallop back to the cemetery before daybreak to return to his grave.

The Legend of Sleepy Hollow's main character is Ichabod Crane, a schoolteacher who believes in witchcraft and evil omens. Ichabod hopes to marry pretty Katrina Van Tassel, daughter of a wealthy farmer, but he has to compete with handsome Brom Bones, who also likes Katrina.

Late one autumn night, as he is returning home from a party at the Van Tassels', Ichabod is followed by a horse and rider. As he crosses the "haunted" bridge where Brom Bones told of being chased by the Headless Horseman, the terrified Ichabod turns and sees the horseman galloping toward him. The horse rears up and, in a fury, the horseman raises his head and hurls it at the schoolteacher.

The next morning, all that remains of Ichabod is his hat, lying next to a shattered pumpkin. Brom Bones, who marries Katrina, laughs each time he hears the tale of how poor Ichabod Crane was carried away in the night by the Headless Horseman of Sleepy Hollow.

Customs, Traditions, Ceremonies

Along with their stories and legends about spooks and things that go bump in the night, immigrants who came to America also brought with them their rituals of Halloween. Over the years, these customs have blended together to form traditions that are uniquely American.

"Trick or treat!"

Trick-or-treating became popular in the United States between 1920 and 1950. It is said to have begun in wealthy areas of the eastern United States and then to have spread to the West and the South by the 1940s. By the 1950s, all American children knew about the new custom, and neighborhood streets were filled with costumed trick-or-treaters on Halloween night.

Ichabod Crane is chased by the Headless Horseman in this illustration from Washington Irving's
Legend of Sleepy Hollow. Irving's 1820 tale shows how a belief in spirits thrived in early America.
Reproduced by permission of AP/Wide World Photos.

For the trick in "trick or treat," pranks were sometimes played on an ill-favored member of the community or on someone who was rude to the trick-or-treaters. Children would mark up windows with a bar of soap; hide tools or take apart outdoor items; smash jack-o'-lanterns; or roll lawns with toilet paper.

A boy masquerading as a pumpkin tests his strength during a fall carnival in Little Rock, Arkansas, in 1999. Many schools have turned away from supernatural Halloween themes and have started to organize parties and fairs for children along seasonal themes. Reproduced by permission of AP/Wide World Photos.

During the 1970s, occasional reports of razor blades, pins, and poison found in children's Halloween candy caused some parents to change the way they allowed their children to trick-or-treat, if they continued to allow it at all. Parents inspected candy thoroughly before children could eat it. Many hospitals offered free candy X-raying on Halloween to help detect any foreign objects that might be in the goodies.

Children were taken only to the homes of friends and family, or were allowed to get treats only from stores, malls, or churches offering "safe" Halloween activities. The scare seemed to lessen in the 1990s, when there were fewer reports of candy tampering; however, most parents still check their children's Halloween candy and throw away any with odd shapes, torn or pierced wrappers, or any unwrapped or homemade treats.

Today, trick-or-treating is a widely accepted Halloween tradition and more than half of American families participate. On Halloween night, a porch light left on and Halloween decorations are signs that the homeowner is participating in Halloween trick-or-treating and will offer

Devil's Night Fires in Detroit

October 30, the eve of Halloween, was called Devil's Night for many years in Detroit, Michigan. The name used to refer to a night of harmless pranks such as soaping windows. During the early 1980s, however, the pranks reached new heights, when fires began breaking out after dark on and around Devil's Night. In 1983, 650 fires were reported on Devil's Night. In 1984, there were 810 fires between October 29 and 31.

By 1985, reports of the Devil's Night fires had spread around the world. Television newspeople from Europe and Japan arrived to photograph the blazes. People fascinated with fire fighting gathered in the city each year for what became known as "the Super Bowl of fire fighting."

By the mid-1980s, Detroit citizens had had enough. They banded together by the thousands to patrol streets and neighborhoods just before Halloween. The effort paid off when the number of Devil's Night fires began to decrease. The city also launched a campaign to clean neighborhoods of trash such as abandoned cars, old tires, and garbage piles that were used to start the fires. Abandoned houses and apartment buildings have also been torn down, and the city limits the sale of gasoline in containers during the days before Devil's Night.

By 1997, Detroit mayor Dennis Archer was hoping to increase the number of citizen patrollers from 34,000 to 35,000. He told the city that Halloween had been given back to Detroit's children. The name *Devil's Night* has been changed to *Angel's Night* because of the help of these volunteers, who call themselves the Motor City Blight Busters. By 1999, the number of fires reported during the Halloween weekend had dropped to 123, which firefighters said was about normal for any weekend in Detroit. The number of fires reported on Devil's Night was less than fifty.

candy. In many neighborhoods, trick-or-treating lasts for a fixed time. It usually begins just before dark and ends at about 8:30 P.M. In cities or rural areas, however, trick-or-treating may go on much later, especially if the holiday falls on a weekend.

Halloween bonfires

Some towns or neighborhoods in the United States still hold bonfires as part of their Halloween celebrations. Everyone gathers around the fire, using this time to visit with friends, drink hot chocolate or apple cider, and show off their Halloween costumes. It is also a way to warm up after trick-or-treating on a cold October night.

Salem, Massachusetts

People remember Salem, Massachusetts, for the gruesome witchcraft trials of 1692, when many innocent people were hanged as witches. Today, Salem has two

Boomers Boost Halloween

Halloween has become a major commercial holiday in the United States, Great Britain, and Canada. Figures show it is celebrated second only to Christmas in terms of retail sales, with dollars spent on costumes, candy, and decorations totaling about $2.5 billion in 1998. It is also second to Christmas in home decorating, with about 65 percent of families decorating for Halloween in 1998. Many writers say this trend has been brought about by "baby boomers" in the United States—adults born between the mid-1940s and mid-1960s—who are reliving their childhood days, when Halloween was at the height of its popularity.

witch museums, a witch village and dungeon, and haunted houses and is becoming one of the most popular places in the United States to celebrate Halloween.

A three-week-long Haunted Happenings festival brought about 500,000 visitors to Salem in 1998. The annual festival began in 1980 and features costumed characters from history; a special midnight ceremony near the Witch Trial Memorial; masked balls; the crowning of a king and queen; the Fright Train, a commuter train from Boston that is decorated for Halloween; and a big parade.

Theme parks celebrate Halloween

A new Halloween tradition is that more and more arenas and theme parks across the United States are getting into the Halloween spirit. Universal Studios in Florida has its elaborate Halloween Horror Nights. Orlando's Scream Park features monsters, spooky creatures, and spine-chilling attractions. There are twenty-five Six Flags theme parks located throughout the United States. They hold a special Halloween event in October called Fright Fest. The Fright Fest features a river of blood, a zombie graveyard, and a hayride of horror. Disney World offers friendly Halloween attractions that are not too scary for small children.

Clothing, Costumes

American children in the 1930s and 1940s wore homemade masks and old clothing or homemade costumes on Halloween. They dressed as clowns, hoboes, pirates, scarecrows, and other characters.

As trick-or-treating gained in popularity during the 1950s and 1960s, children dressed as witches, devils, ghosts, goblins, skeletons, jack-o'-lanterns, cats and dogs, tigers, elephants, fairy princesses, and cowboys, with the familiar hobo, scarecrow, and clown remaining favorites as well. Most costumes were still homemade, perhaps with the addition of a purchased rubber mask. Parents later began to buy patterns and sew their children fancier costumes such as Cinderella, Superman, Batman and Cat Woman, and other popular characters from television and movies.

Influenced by movies and TV, older children and adults began to wear costumes that were more realistic and scary. Fake blood, scars, wounds, and severed body parts became popular, and characters such as the mummy, werewolf, vampire, Frankenstein, and the ax murderer (or his victim), roamed the streets on Halloween night.

I want to bite you ... in the wallet!

Halloween costumes continue to reflect popular culture. Each year, characters from the latest hit movie, the year's big political scandal, the hottest rock group, or favorite TV commercial appear at Halloween. Trick-or-treaters and partygoers sometimes also dress as objects, like the Statue of Liberty, a piece of furniture, or a food item.

With increasing adult participation at Halloween parties and in Halloween parades in large cities such as New York and San Francisco, costumes are becoming even more elaborate. According to one source, adults are spending as much as $1,000 on costumes and makeup. Hollywood costumers are selling special contact lenses, false teeth, artificial body parts, wigs, jewelry, and clothing to those who want to look exactly like their favorite Halloween character.

Many parade participants design their own costumes and props, sometimes spending months creating them. Halloween is being compared with Mardi Gras in terms of its parades, which increase in size and participation every year.

Foods, Recipes

Because Halloween is associated with the fall harvest, many of the foods served at traditional Halloween parties are those harvested around this time of year. Apples have always been a Halloween favorite, served baked or coated with caramel, or in the form of hot apple cider. Popcorn balls are another traditional Halloween treat, as are nuts and

Pumpkin Cookies

Ingredients

1½ cups brown sugar, packed
½ cup shortening
2 eggs
1 can pumpkin (1 pound)
2¾ cups flour, sifted
1 tablespoon baking powder
1 teaspoon cinnamon
¾ teaspoon nutmeg
½ teaspoon salt
¼ teaspoon ginger
1 cup raisins
¾ cup pecans, chopped

Directions

1. Mix sugar, shortening, eggs, and pumpkin thoroughly in a large bowl.
2. Sift flour, baking powder, cinnamon, nutmeg, salt, and ginger and add to pumpkin mixture. Blend well. Add raisins and pecans.
3. Drop batter by teaspoonsful onto ungreased baking sheets.
4. Bake at 400 degrees for 12 to 15 minutes or until lightly browned.

Makes about 6 dozen cookies

nut candies. And, of course, anything made from pumpkin.

Candy in all forms plays a big role in Halloween celebrations. Traditional Halloween sweets include candy pumpkins and corn kernels and peanut butter chews wrapped in orange or black paper. Children love to take home bags filled with many kinds of candy given by neighbors and friends. Some adults choose to give more healthful treats, such as granola bars or fruit chews.

Arts, Crafts, Games

Bobbing for apples was, and still is, a popular activity for Halloween parties. In the nineteenth and early twentieth centuries in the United States, it was also very popular at public fall carnivals and school or church parties held around Halloween. Apples are an important part of the fall harvest in many parts of the world and have been associated with harvest festivals since the time of the Celts and the Romans in Europe. The game was probably brought to America by Scottish and Irish immigrants.

To play bobbing for apples, a dozen or more apples are placed in a large metal tub. Players have their hands tied behind their backs. They kneel on the floor around the tub and each player tries to grab an apple with his teeth—no hands allowed. Players duck their heads under the water, pushing an apple to the bottom of the tub with their mouths, then sink their teeth in and come up to win a prize.

In another version of bobbing for apples, the apple is suspended from a string by its stem and swung from a doorway. Players try to grab the apple with their teeth.

For More Information

Bannatyne, Lesley Pratt. *Halloween: An American Holiday, An American History*. New York: Facts on File, 1990.

Santino, Jack, ed. *Halloween and Other Festivals of Death and Life*. Knoxville: University of Tennessee Press, 1994.

Web sites
"Ben and Jerry's Halloween Page." [Online] http://www.benjerry.com/halloween/index.html (accessed on February 11, 2000).

"The History of Halloween." [Online] http://historychannel.com/cgi-bin/framed.cgi (accessed on February 11, 2000).

UNICEF's Home Page. [Online] http://www.unicef.org (accessed on February 1, 2000).

Halloween and Festivals of the Dead Sources

Beimler, Rosalind Rosoff. *The Days of the Dead (Los Dias de Los Muertos)*. San Francisco: Collins, 1991, pp. 14–25.

Dineen, Jacqueline. *Feasts and Festivals*. Philadelphia: Chelsea House, 1999.

DuVal, Linda. "That's the Spirit: Halloween Isn't Just For Kids Anymore; It's Now a Big-Time Grownup Thing." *The Gazette*, October 29, 1998.

Griffin, Robert H., and Ann H. Shurgin, eds. *The Folklore of World Holidays*. 2nd ed. Detroit, Mich.: Gale, 1999, pp. 279–82, 457–62, 604–13, 636–41.

Henderson, Helene, and Sue Ellen Thompson. *Holidays, Festivals, and Celebrations of the World Dictionary*. 2nd ed. Detroit, Mich.: Omnigraphics, 1997, pp. 9, 178–79, 196, 305, 344.

Hutton, Ronald. *The Stations of the Sun: A History of the Ritual Year in Britain*. Oxford: Oxford University Press, 1996, pp. 379–84.

Latsch, Marie-Luise. *Traditional Chinese Festivals*. Singapore: Graham Brash, 1988.

Law, Ruth. *Pacific Light Cooking*. New York: Donald I. Fine, 1998, pp. 26–27.

Lee, Bobbie. "Chinese Festivals in San Jose." *Asian Week*, April 22, 1994.

Let's Celebrate, compiled by John Foster. Oxford: Oxford University Press, 1989, p. 40.

Pitts, Lilla Belle, Mabelle Glenn, Lorrain E. Watters, and Louis G. Wersen, eds. *Singing Together.* Boston: Ginn and Company, 1960, p. 107.

Santino, Jack. *All Around the Year: Holidays and Celebrations in American Life.* Chicago: University of Illinois Press, 1994, pp. 148–67.

Scalora, Salvatore. "Celebrating the Spirits' Return." *Américas* 47, no. 5 (1995): 32–41.

Thompson, Sue Ellen, ed. *Holiday Symbols 1998.* Detroit, Mich.: Omnigraphics, 1998, pp. 61–64, 164–71, 191–93, 330–32.

Webb, Lois Sinaiko. *Holidays of the World Cookbook for Students.* Phoenix, Ariz.: Oryx Press, 1995, pp. 112, 154.

Web sites

"A Brief History of Halloween." [Online] http://dcls.org/x/archives/halloween.html (accessed on February 7, 2000).

"Day of the Dead." [Online] http://www.nacnet.org/assunta/dead.htm (accessed on February 9, 2000).

"The Days of the Dead." [Online] http://www.foodwine.com/food/egg/egg1096/daydead.html (accessed on February 9, 2000).

"Festivals and Folk Arts: Tomb Sweeping Day." *Taiwan Republic of China.* [Online] http://www.houstoncul.org/festival/tomb.txt (accessed on February 9, 2000).

"Nos Galan Gaeaf." *Welsh Cultural Traditions. [Online]* http://www.britannia.com/wales/culture1.html (accessed on February 9, 2000).

"Sugar Skulls." [Online] http://www.sat.lib.tx.us/html/DeadDay/sugar.htm (accessed on February 10, 2000).

Index

Italic type indicates volume numbers;
boldface type indicates entries and their page numbers;
(ill.) indicates illustrations;
(box) indicates information found in sidebar boxes.

Y

Yaa Asantewaa *3:* 284
Yalanchi (Stuffed Peppers) *4:* 413, 414 (recipe)
Yams *3:* 285, *4:* 429, 446-52
Yankee Doodle *3:* 268, 318
Yasothon *1:* 10–11
Yes, Virginia, There Is a Santa Claus *1:* 120 (box)
Yom Ha'atzmaut *3:* 257, 287–99
Yom Kippur *4:* 341, 379, 386–87, 403
Yorktown, Virginia *3:* 313
Yoruba *3:* 322, 446
Yuan Xiao *4:* 356

Yule *1:* 116–28
Yule log *1:* 99

Z

Zion *3:* 266–677, 288, 291–92
Ziripot *1:* 20 (ill.)
Zorrilla y Moral, José *2:* 219
Zoroastrianism *4:* 372
Zulu *3:* 321, 330
Zurich, Switzerland *1:* 71 (ill.)